Centerville Library
Washington-Centerville Public Library
Cen

D0725659

Legendary
COCKTAILS

Legendary
COCKTAILS

NH
NEW
HOLLAND

First published in 2002 by New Holland Publishers Ltd
London • Cape Town • Sydney • Auckland
www.newhollandpublishers.com

86 Edgware Road
London
W2 2EA
United Kingdom

14 Aquatic Drive
Frenchs Forest
NSW 2086
Australia

80 McKenzie Street
Cape Town
8001
South Africa

218 Lake Road
Northcote
Auckland
New Zealand

Copyright © 2002 New Holland Publishers (UK) Ltd
Copyright © 2002 in text: David Biggs
Copyright © 2002 in photographs:
Struik Image Library/Ryno with the exception of individual photographers and/or their agents as listed below

All rights reserved. No part of this publication may be reproduced, stored in a retrieval system or transmitted, in any form or by any means, electronic, mechanical, photocopying, recording or otherwise, without the prior written permission of the publishers and copyright holders.

ISBN 1 84330 374 4 (UK)
ISBN 1 86966 018 8 (NZ)

PUBLISHING MANAGER Claudia Dos Santos
MANAGING EDITOR Simon Pooley
DESIGN CONCEPT Petal Palmer
PROJECT DESIGNER Geraldine Cupido
EDITORIAL ASSISTANCE Leizel Brown
PRODUCTION Myrna Collins
STYLIST Sylvie Hurford

Reproduction by Hirt & Carter Cape (Pty) Ltd
Printed and bound by Craft Print (Pte) Ltd, Singapore

10 9 8 7 6 5 4 3

CONTENTS

INTRODUCTION

No-one knows for certain where the word "cocktail" originated, although many people have their favourite theories.

One is that the name was derived from a mixed drink called a "Coquetel", served to French officers in the southern States of America during the American War of Independence 1775–1783.

Another theory is that the cocktail was the product of the American Prohibition era, but this is not so as cocktails were mentioned in a magazine article as far back as 1806, long before Prohibition was introduced.

The British claim the word comes from the dregs drawn from the very bottom of barrels of spirits and known as "cock-tailings".

My own favourite version is that they were the invention of an enterprising Irish-American innkeeper, Betsy Flanagan, who decorated her creations with gaily coloured feathers from fighting cocks. Apparently, a very appreciative French customer found himself so delighted by his unusual drink that he raised his glass and toasted: "*Vive le cocktail*".

Whatever your personal favourite, there is little doubt that the cocktail reached its peak of fame during the 1920s, when Prohibition was in full swing in America. (The one factor that did more to promote the popularity of the cocktail than any other was the enactment of the 18th Amendment to the American Constitution in 1919. It ushered in 13 years of total prohibition on the sale of alcoholic drinks in the United States of America.) In order to stay one jump ahead of the beady-eyed police, the owners of speakeasies disguised the appearance of alcoholic drinks (and the rather rough taste of bad moonshine liquor), and the cocktail soared in popularity. Of course, the fact that alcohol was illegal added to the glamour of the cocktail bar.

PROHIBITION

Prohibition was not a new concept in the US. The State of Kansas had prohibited the sale of liquor back in the 1880s and many other rural areas had vociferous groups that condemned the "demon alcohol". Once the idea had spread that alcohol was a wicked, sinful thing, it was difficult for any public figure to state otherwise.

The Prohibitionists swept the board and the new law came into force in 1920 – the "Cocktail Age" had begun.

Give any commodity a rarity value and its price will rise. Bootlegging – the illegal sale of alcohol – became lucrative business. Soon shiploads of illicit booze from Europe and South America were being smuggled throughout the United States. Profits were enormous.

A long coastline made effective patrol impossible, and smugglers developed ingenious ways to land their wares. The liquor came ashore in anything that floated and was unlikely to attract the attention of the US Coast Guard.

It was permitted to obtain whisky for "medicinal" purposes, and many doctors grew rich writing out prescriptions for their ailing patients. It was also possible to import denatured alcohol for

Moonshine was the term used for illicitly distilled whisky. Here, confiscated barrels are waiting to be destroyed.

industrial use. It is estimated that some 57 million litres of this alcohol was diverted. The alcohol was cooked to remove poisonous chemicals before the bootlegger added flavouring and colouring agents. The product, sold as whiskey, gin or rum, was often very dangerous, resulting in illness, paralysis, blindness and even death.

By the late 1920s the industry had become quite organized. Crude stills, established in many remote areas, distilled liquor from corn syrup, malt and yeast. The resulting booze, known to be dangerous, was given names such as "coffin varnish", "squirrel juice", "rotgut" and "strike-me-dead". Sometimes it did.

This dreadful liquor was sold in speakeasies, and most popular were those establishments that found ways of making it palatable. They mixed it with fruit juices, added syrups and decorated it with slices of fruit. Bartenders became legends on the reputation of their cocktail recipes.

Of course, no lucrative industry like this remains untouched by crime for long, and soon organized gangs took over the distribution of illegal drink from private entrepreneurs.

It was big money; it was a dangerous game. Gangsters fought and died protecting the right to sell in their hardwon territories. Competition was ruthlessly eliminated by gang bosses like the notorious Al Capone. It was only when Prohibition was repealed in 1933 that the liquor industry settled down to legal respectability – and the gangs lost their reason to exist.

Prohibition had played a pivotal role in achieving exactly the opposite of what its protagonists wanted. At the end of the Prohibition era, Americans were once again able to buy "normal" drinks that didn't require additives to mask the flavour, and cocktails declined in popularity. Who needs something that is freely available?

In recent years, however, there has been renewed interest, and bartenders around the world are inventing new and tempting drinks to delight the palate and the eye. Americans now call an expert cocktail creator a "mixologist". Let's raise our glasses and drink a toast to the mixologists of the world.

During Prohibition, alcohol was sold illegally in establishments known as speakeasies, probably so named because regulars would knock softly on the door, and then wait until a little slot was opened before uttering the password and being admitted. They had to "speak easy" in order to get inside.

STOCKING UP

There are thousands of alcoholic drinks available and no-one can be expected to stock all of them. Every bar should, however, have a basic range of spirits, as well as mixers and garnishes that can be adapted to suit your needs.

I have not listed wines in any detail here, because they are a vast subject in themselves that can (and does) fill many books. The basics are a dry white wine and a serviceable red blend.

The following list acts as a guide for the beginner bartender.

THE SPIRITS

Brandy or cognac
Gin
Vodka
Rum (dark and light)
Scotch whisky
Bourbon
Tequila
Vermouth, dry and sweet
Sparkling wine (dry)
Dry white wine
    (Sauvignon Blanc is a safe bet)
Dry red wine
    (an inexpensive blended red will do)
Triple Sec
Your own choice of liqueurs

THE MIXERS

Club soda
Colas and Ginger ale
Indian tonic water
Tomato juice
Fruit juices
Mineral water
Grenadine
Angostura bitters

SAUCES, SPICES AND GARNISHES

Maraschino cherries
Olives (green and black)
Cocktail onions
Lemons
Limes
Oranges
Nutmeg
Caster sugar
Tabasco sauce
Worcestershire sauce
Sugar syrup (gomme)
Sour syrup
    (a mixture of lemon and lime juice)

AND FINALLY

Ice, ice and more ice, cubes, crushed and cracked. You can never have too much ice in a good cocktail bar.

MEASURES

In the cocktail recipes in this book, the use of actual quantities has been avoided as almost every country has its own particular set of measurements. Some bartenders prefer to use gills, while others measure in fluid ounces or centilitres. The use of conversions would have made this book rather clumsy and confusing to the reader. It's far easier to work in proportion, we believe.

"One part" of vodka to "two parts of orange juice" will taste the same whether the parts are teaspoons or tot measures. The use of proportions rather than quantities allows you, the reader, to determine the size of your drink. You can also make up more than one drink at a time by substituting a coffee mug (or a bucket!) for your usual bar measuring jigger.

EQUIPMENT

For many readers, cocktails will be a passing fancy – a one-party stand – and there's nothing wrong with that. If this is what you are doing you'll probably find all the equipment you need already in your home. You can use ordinary kitchen tools and utensils to create almost any cocktail.

For those who wish to take cocktail making a little more seriously, it's worth getting a few accessories that will make the task more enjoyable and certainly enhance your reputation as a host. Always buy good-quality equipment. They should look good, feel good and do the job for which they are designed. Here's a short list of items the budding home bartender would need:

• **A sharp knife**
• **An ice bucket:** The traditional ice bucket is made of metal, but in hot climates it might be better to have one with an insulated lining.
• **Ice tongs**
• **A measure:** It doesn't really matter what size measure you use, as long as you use the same one for all the ingredients of your drink; they are also known as "jiggers" or "tot measures". It may be

a good idea to have two measures, one being twice the capacity of the other.
• **Corkscrews:** There are many different kinds available. There is the "screwpull" range, which has the spirals with a non-stick coating; the "waiter's friend", which has an arm that rests on the rim of the bottle to provide leverage; the "wing" corkscrew, which has two arms that are depressed to lift the cork from the bottle neck; the "Ah So", which is a cork lifter rather than a corkscrew, with two slender prongs of spring steel that are slid down the sides of the cork and then carefully twisted out (it is designed to handle corks that have become crumbly with age); and the "cork pump", a hand-operated pump attached to a hollow needle which is pushed down through the cork.
• **A bottle opener**
• **A cocktail shaker**
• **A bar glass with strainer**
• **A water pitcher**

The following are useful if you intend mixing drinks in substantial quantities.
• **A bar spoon**
• **Cloths**
• **Bar towels**
• **Damp wiping cloth**

DECORATING YOUR DRINKS

The charming thing about cocktails is that they are designed to please all the senses. They should not only taste good, but smell and look good too.

Conscientious bartenders will take care to ensure that their creations are a feast for the eye as well as the palate, but garnish should never dominate the cocktail. A concoction bristling with fruit, paper umbrellas, swizzle sticks and bright-blue plastic ice cubes simply looks a mess. By adding just the right touch of garnish, a clever bartender can give an indication of the flavour to be expected. A twist of lemon or lime, for example, will tell the drinker to be prepared for a crisp, slightly tangy drink. A maraschino cherry or ball of watermelon on a cocktail stick would indicate sweet and syrupy.

Garnishes like sprigs of mint add to the flavour or aroma of the drink, while there are certain cocktails that traditionally require a specific garnish, such as the olive in a dry martini.

A pretty touch is added by serving the cocktail in a glass with a frosted rim. This is done by wetting the rim with water or egg white and then dipping it into a saucer of fine sugar. (In the case of a margarita, the rim of the glass is frosted with salt.)

Some drinks are best sipped through a straw. Unless the glass is a very tall one, a short straw is best. Trim off as much of a full-length straw as you require.

THE ROLE OF FRUIT

All cocktail recipes can be enhanced by the addition of a slice or two of fresh fruit dropped into the glass, or a chunk of fruit threaded onto a cocktail stick, if the mood is right.

Fruit can play a number of roles in the creation of a perfect cocktail for a specific occasion. Remember also that a good cocktail should not only taste good but look good – and fruit is ideal for adding eye appeal.

Appropriate fruits, when in season, can provide an exciting base for a cocktail. Bananas, melons, peaches, apricots and a variety of other soft fruit can be liquidized in a blender to create a delicious fruit purée. The addition of vodka, rum or brandy will create a superb and refreshing drink.

HANGOVER CURES

Sooner or later, every enthusiastic drinker will encounter this demon: the hangover. Chances are you'll blame it on the soda water, the peanuts or the suspect quality of the cheese straws – but seldom, if ever, on the alcohol you consumed the night before.

It is interesting to hear how many people claim that they cannot handle champagne because it "gives them such a hangover". But just think of the occasions on which this

Marlene Dietrich looking the worse for wear in Blonde Venus.

beverage is enjoyed. They are usually celebrations such as weddings, birthdays, engagements and so on. And the evening often begins with a beer or two, continues with a few cocktails and then a glass or two of wine with the meal. When it comes to speech time, we break out the champagne to drink the toasts. And we always blame the champers, not the beers, cocktails or wine, for the hangover that will inevitably follow the next morning.

The hangover is a malady as old as alcohol itself and many cures have been prescribed. Few of them actually work, but when you're feeling as dreadful as that, you'll try anything. Even death seems a happy alternative to the pounding, sick head and stomach of a hangover.

One of the worst aspects is that a hangover seldom evokes much sympathy from anybody else. The general attitude is one of "well, you have only yourself to blame". While this may, of course, be perfectly true, it is not the sort of statement that makes the sufferer feel any better. Anyone in the throes of a hangover requires much sympathy and understanding and – above all – total silence.

The ancient Egyptians believed that boiled cabbage would do the trick. The Assyrians recommended ground-up swallows' beaks blended with myrrh. Where one was supposed to find a swallow's beak the morning after a rough party, history does not relate.

In South America some ancient Indian tribes believed the best remedy was to tie the sufferer tightly in his hammock like a mummy and leave him alone until he was ready to face the world.

I believe the old Scots thought the best way was to wrap the patient very tightly in an oxhide and stow him out of sight behind a waterfall.

Many famous authors have described their own favourite hangover remedies. One of these was Thackeray, who wrote: "To this truth I can vouch as a man; there is no headache in the world like that caused by Vauxhall Punch." He does not describe the punch in detail, but later writes: "Small beer was the only drink with which unhappy gentlemen soothed the fever of their previous night's potation." Small beer, incidentally, was made by adding water to the mash left after the real beer had been brewed, and then fermenting it again. It was a thin and cheap drink, and rather watery.

Lord Byron, in his epic satire Don Juan, says the following:

"Get very drunk; and when
You wake with a headache,
you shall see what then.
Ring for your valet –
bid him quickly bring
Some hock and soda water,
then you'll know
A pleasure worth Xerxes,
the greatest king;
For not the blest sherbert,
sublimed with snow,
Nor the first sparkle of the desert spring,
Nor Burgundy in all its sunset glow
After long travel, ennui, love or slaughter,
Vie with that draught
of hock and soda water."

Byron was, in fact, writing about the drink we today call a spritzer.

Some people believe there's merit in the old "hair of the dog that bit you" story. In other words, cure the malady with a quick shot of whatever caused it in the first place. This, of course, does raise quite serious problems if you were bitten by a whole pack of dogs of different breeds.

Some hangover sufferers recommend such odd mixtures as raw egg liberally laced with Worcestershire sauce.

Actress Tallulah Bankhead recommended Black Velvet, a mixture of champagne and stout, as a hangover cure, but adds, rather honestly: *"Don't be swindled into believing there's any cure for a hangover. I've tried them all. Time alone can stay it."*

In his book *Clement Freud's Book of Hangovers*, British ex-politician, chef and bon viveur Clement Freud makes the following suggestion: *"Drink plenty of water, milk or fruit juice before, during and after drinking alcohol."*

Plenty of water certainly does help to relieve the suffering, and a couple of headache tablets swallowed immediately before going to bed – if you can remember, at that fuzzy stage of the evening (or morning), to take them – will definitely reduce the pain that sets in when you arise again.

In America, the Prairie Oyster (*see recipe opposite page*) is often recommended, but frankly, if you can bear to look a Prairie Oyster in the eye when you have a hangover, then you are a better man than I am.

Here is a selection of recipes. Read them while you're sober.

PICK-ME-UP GENTLY

This gentle drink for the morning after is unlikely to cause any further damage. It is also completely non-alcoholic and many users swear that it settles the stomach as fast as anything else they've tried (which may be damning with faint praise, but it's worth a try).

- Ice cubes
- The juice of half a lemon
- Two teaspoons of Worcestershire sauce
- Soda water

- Place two ice cubes in a high-ball glass (oh, any glass will do as long as it's handy without any fuss) and add the lemon juice and Worcestershire sauce.
- Top it up with soda water and sip very quietly.
- Avoid human contact.

PRAIRIE OYSTER

The Prairie Oyster, sometimes called Mountain Oyster, is one of the oldest hangover cocktails around, but the strong flavours are daunting to some.

- Ice cubes
- One generous measure of brandy
- Two teaspoons cider vinegar
- A dessertspoon of Worcestershire sauce
- A teaspoon of tomato sauce
- Half a teaspoon of Angostura bitters
- The yolk of a fresh egg
- Cayenne pepper

- Place five ice cubes in a cocktail shaker, add the brandy, vinegar, Worcestershire sauce, tomato sauce and bitters.
- Strain into a lowball glass and add ice cubes to bring it to the top of the glass.
- Carefully float the unbroken egg yolk on top and sprinkle lightly with cayenne pepper.
- Traditionally this concoction should be downed in a single, brave gulp.

POLYNESIAN PICK-ME-UP

This remedy relies on savoury flavours combined with tart, acid fruit juices to affect a cure. Look, nobody is saying these are pleasant drinks. They are, essentially, medicine.

- Crushed ice
- One part vodka
- Four parts pineapple juice
- Half teaspoon curry powder
- A teaspoon of lemon juice
- Two dashes Tabasco sauce
- Cayenne pepper

- Place half a cup of crushed ice and all the ingredients except the cayenne pepper in a blender.
- Blend for about 10 seconds and pour it into a lowball glass.
- Dust the surface lightly with cayenne pepper and drink in a single, shuddering gulp.

BRANDY

Brandy, that warming spirit distilled from wine, is produced in many forms around the world. Best known are the heady cognacs and armagnacs of France (probably considered by purists to be too noble to be used in anything as frivolous as a cocktail), but fine **brandy** is also distilled in many other countries, including Germany, Greece, America and South Africa.

Top-quality brandies are produced in copper pot stills, while the more commercial brands are made in continuous patent stills. Several countries have regulations stating what proportion of a **brandy** may be produced in a continuous still and how long the distilled product must be matured in oak vats before being released for sale.

The tradition of maturing **brandy** in oak goes back to the 15th century, when an alchemist allegedly took his precious barrel of aqua vitae and buried it in his yard to keep it out of the hands of soldiers about to attack his village. The poor man died in the attack and it was only years later that the barrel was discovered. Half the liquor had evaporated by then, but the remaining nectar was found to be incredibly rich and smooth.

Brandy has long been considered a man's drink. Samuel Johnson's 18th-century philosophy was: "Claret is the liquor for boys, port for men: but he who aspires to be a hero must drink **brandy**." Times have certainly changed, and today **brandy** is a spirit enjoyed as much by women as by men.

B & B

B & B is a natural combination, as Benedictine is a herb-flavoured liqueur based on brandy and originally made by Benedictine monks who claimed it had fine medicinal qualities, which it probably does.

- Ice cubes
- One part brandy
- One part Benedictine
- A twist of lime

- Place two or three ice cubes in a bar glass and add the brandy and Benedictine.
- Stir well and then strain the combination into a small cocktail glass.
- Garnish with the twist of lime.

BULL'S MILK

Milk is traditionally the drink for children, so it is unlikely that the rough, tough gangsters of the Prohibition era would have accepted it willingly. But Bull's Milk is another matter. The bull is the symbol of bravery and awesome power – and no macho male could quibble with a glass of that.

- Ice cubes
- One part brandy
- One cup of milk
- Sugar syrup
- Grated nutmeg
- Finely ground cinnamon

- Place four or five ice cubes in a cocktail shaker and add the brandy, milk and sugar syrup to taste.
- Shake the mixture well and then strain it into a highball glass.
- Sprinkle the nutmeg and cinnamon over it and serve immediately.

B & B COLLINS

The B & B can be extended to make a B & B Collins simply by adding club soda water, but that would be very unadventurous. Rather, try this little variation.

- Two parts brandy
- The juice of half a lemon
- A teaspoon of sugar syrup
- Crushed ice
- Club soda water
- One part Benedictine
- A slice of lemon

- Mix the brandy, lemon juice and sugar syrup in a bar glass after adding three scoops of crushed ice.
- Strain it into a chilled lowball glass and top with soda water.
- Now carefully float the Benedictine on the surface and garnish with the slice of lemon.

BLACKSMITH COCKTAIL

There's a rough Irish drink called a "Blacksmith" which consists, predictably, of half a pint each of Guinness stout and barley wine, probably best drunk and enjoyed in the glow of the blacksmith's forge. Our Blacksmith Cocktail, however, is better suited to the cocktail bar.

- Ice cubes
- One part brandy
- One part Drambuie
- One part crème de café

- Place four or five ice cubes in a bar mixing glass, add all the ingredients and stir well.
- Serve ungarnished on the rocks in a lowball glass or you could also use a whisky glass.

B & B Collins (**opposite right**), *a longer, cooler variation of the B & B, and Blacksmith Cocktail* (**opposite left**), *a smooth blend of Drambuie and crème de café.*

*The brandy cocktail (**above centre and right**) comes in several versions. It's fun to find your own favourite. The Sidecar (**above left**) is one of many cocktail classics that had its origins in the legendary Harry's New York Bar in Paris.*

THE SIDECAR

The 1920s, the golden age of the cocktail, was also the golden age of motoring. The novelty of the horseless carriage had not yet worn off and automobiles were different and dashing. And the most dashing of all the knights of the road were the gallant fellows who dared to ride motorcycles.

The Sidecar is said to be named after a rather eccentric military man who used to arrive at Harry's New York Bar in Paris in the sidecar of a chauffeur-driven motorcycle.

- Ice cubes
- One and a half parts brandy

- One part Cointreau
- One part fresh lemon juice (or more to taste)

- Place four ice cubes in a mixing glass, pour the ingredients over the ice and stir well.
- Strain into a cocktail glass and serve.

BRANDY COCKTAIL

There must be dozens of cocktails called, simply, "Brandy Cocktail". One bartender's reference book on my shelf contains no fewer than eight completely different brandy cocktails.

Here are two of my favourites for you to try:

VERSION 1
- Ice cubes
- One part brandy
- One part dry vermouth
- A dash of Angostura bitters
- Lemon zest
- A cocktail cherry

- Place five ice cubes in a bar mixing glass and add the brandy, vermouth and bitters.

- Stir gently and strain into a cocktail glass.
- Add the lemon zest.
- Garnish with a cocktail cherry on a stick.

VERSION 2
- Ice cubes
- Two parts brandy
- One part vermouth
- One part Grand Marnier
- Angostura bitters
- Orange peel

- Place four or five ice cubes in a bar mixing glass and pour the brandy, vermouth and Grand Marnier over them. Stir well.
- Add two dashes of bitters to an empty cocktail glass and swirl it round to completely coat the inside of the glass.
- Strain the mixture from the mixing glass into the cocktail glass.
- Squeeze the orange peel over the glass to add zest and aroma.
- Serve ungarnished.

EGGNOG

Traditionally this was the drink served in English country homes on Christmas morning to keep out the chill. The eggnog probably derived its name from the term "noggin", which was a small glass of strong beer. Some folk enjoyed this with an egg beaten in to thicken it. Nowadays we prefer brandy and rum instead of beer. It's one of the few cocktails in this collection that does not involve ice.

- One part brandy
- One part dark rum
- One fresh egg
- A dash of sweet syrup
- Five parts full-cream milk
- Whole nutmeg

- Place the brandy, rum, egg and the sweet syrup in a shaker and shake vigorously to create a creamy consistency.
- Strain it into a highball glass, add the milk and stir it gently.
- Grate a sprinkling of nutmeg over it and serve the drink at room temperature.

STINGER

This very old cocktail recipe has its origins in the days of American Prohibition and has become a true classic. Originally it was served "straight up" but most people now prefer to sip it on the rocks. It's a good way to get a party rolling as fast as possible; one or two Stingers and your guests are almost guaranteed to be in a jolly mood.

- Ice cubes
- Two parts brandy
- One part white crème de menthe

- Place six ice cubes in a cocktail shaker, add the brandy and crème de menthe.
- Shake well and strain into a chilled cocktail glass.
- Serve ungarnished or with a sprig of mint if preferred.

THE INTERNATIONAL

One of the reasons this cocktail got its name is that it combines the flavours typical of several national drinks.

- Crushed ice
- Two parts cognac
- Half a part vodka
- Half a part ouzo
- Half a part Cointreau

Place two scoops of crushed ice in a bar mixing glass and add the cognac, vodka, ouzo and Cointreau.

Stir well and strain into a chilled cocktail glass.

Serve ungarnished, or decorate with a tiny flag.

WIDOW'S KISS

The spirit that is distilled from apple cider in the New England area of America is known as applejack. It is more or less the same as Calvados from France. This apple brandy has a hefty alcohol content of about 45%.

- Crushed ice
- One part applejack
- One part Benedictine
- Half part yellow chartreuse
- A dash of Angostura bitters
- A fresh strawberry

- Place a scoop of crushed ice in a cocktail shaker and add the applejack, Benedictine, chartreuse and bitters.
- Shake well and strain into a chilled cocktail glass.
- Decorate by floating the fresh strawberry on the top.

THE ROLLS ROYCE

Perhaps this drink was designed to be served in the back of a Rolls as the chauffeur drives you silently through the British countryside.

- Crushed ice
- One part cognac
- One part Cointreau
- One part orange juice

- Place three scoops of crushed ice in a cocktail shaker and add the cognac, Cointreau and the part orange juice.
- Shake well, then strain the contents into a chilled cocktail glass.
- Serve ungarnished.

STEEPLEJACK

Calvados is distilled apple cider and is a popular spirit in parts of France, such as Normandy, where apple cider is the drink of the area. In other parts of the world it is sold as apple brandy or applejack.

- One part Calvados (oh, okay, applejack then)
- One and a half parts chilled apple juice
- One and a half parts of soda water
- One teaspoon of lime juice
- Ice cubes
- A slice of lemon

- Pour the Calvados, apple juice, soda water and lime juice into a bar glass and stir gently.
- Pour the mixture into a highball glass and add ice to fill it.
- Garnish with a slice of lemon.

Rolls Royce (**opposite front**), *a cocktail as elegant as the car after which it is named, and Steeplejack* (**opposite back**), *a long, cool drink with a distinct apple flavour.*

"Claret is the liquor for boys,
port for men; but he who aspires to be
a hero must drink brandy."

Samuel Johnson

CHARLESTON

The Charleston was one of the most popular dances during the Prohibition era and typified the new, rather risqué age, when young ladies could show an ankle in public and dresses were figure-hugging and sheer rather than elaborate and all-concealing. This drink would have appealed to the liberated young women of the time. It appeals just as much today.

- One part mandarin Napoleon liqueur
- One part cherry brandy
- Ice cubes
- Lemonade to taste

- Place the mandarin Napoleon and cherry brandy in a bar glass and stir well.
- Fill a highball glass with ice cubes and pour the cocktail over them.
- Top up with lemonade and serve.

OLD OXFORD UNIVERSITY PUNCH

Most of the Oxford academic year is in winter when the air is chilly in the draughty old college buildings. No doubt many a long and otherwise boring tutorial has been made more bearable by a warming mug of punch.

- One cup of brown sugar
- Boiling water
- Three cups of lemon juice
- One bottle of cognac
- One bottle dark Demerara rum
- Cinnamon sticks and whole cloves

- Dissolve the sugar in the boiling water in a saucepan on low heat on the stove. Keep it hot, but ensure it does not boil at any stage. Add the lemon juice and cognac when the sugar has dissolved.

- Pour in most of the rum, leaving about half a cup in the bottle.

- Shortly before serving, place the remaining rum in a ladle and heat over a flame. Light the rum in the ladle, pour the flaming spirit onto the surface of the punch and serve. If flames are still flickering, extinguish them with the lid of the saucepan.

APPLE GINGER PUNCH

Ginger has been used in many drinks to add a glowing touch of spicy warmth. Here we combine the flavours of ginger beer and ginger wine to make a most refreshing party drink.

- A large block of ice
- One bottle of Calvados
- Half a cup of maraschino liqueur
- Half a cup of Kirsch
- A bottle of ginger wine
- Three cups of pineapple or grapefruit juice
- Four apples (red or green)
- Three bottles of ginger beer

Place the ice in a punch bowl and pour the Calvados (apple-jack), maraschino, Kirsch, ginger wine and fruit juice over it. Cut the apples into wedge-shaped slices and float them in the punch.

Shortly before serving, add the ginger beer to the bowl.

GIN

Gin is probably the most commonly used base for cocktails, including the most famous cocktail of them all, the martini. The original **gin** used in Prohibition cocktails was known as bathtub **gin**, as it was often concocted illegally in the bathtub and bore little if any resemblance to the elegantly fragrant **gin** that we know today.

Official definitions of **gin** describe it as a "neutral, rectified spirit distilled from any grain, potato or beet and flavoured with juniper". This would seem to give the distillers a fairly wide range of possibilities and indeed, there are several styles of the white spirit, all falling under the general category of "**gin**".

Each producer has a closely guarded recipe for **gin**, with juniper berries as a base, but sometimes also including a touch of coriander, angelica root and seed, dried orange and lemon peel, cassia bark and orris powder.

Sloe **gin** is one of the better-known styles of **gin** and has been flavoured with sloe, which is the small, dark fruit of the blackthorn. The name lends itself to some interesting and sometimes risqué cocktails, like the 'Sloe, Comfortable Screw" which is, of course, made up of sloe **gin**, Southern Comfort and the basic screwdriver ingredients.

There are probably as many variations of the popular martini as there are bartenders, each with his or her own recipe. The question, too, is whether a martini should be shaken or stirred. Here are a few variations of that famous cocktail.

Above from left to right: *Dry Martini, Medium Martini, Sweet Martini. Martinis come in many forms – the difference is usually in the sweetness of the vermouth and the right choice of garnish.*

MEDIUM MARTINI

If you use the same measure, the Medium Martini will end up rather more alcoholic than the other two. Traditionally this elegant cocktail is served without any garnish.

- Ice cubes
- One part gin
- One part dry vermouth
- One part sweet vermouth

Place eight ice cubes in a cocktail mixing glass and pour the gin and both measures of vermouth over them.

Stir well and then strain into a martini glass.

DRY MARTINI

The dry martini is undoubtedly the most famous cocktail in the world and every bartender has a favourite way of making it. This is just one of many martini variations.

- Ice cubes
- One part gin
- One part dry vermouth
- A green olive

  Place four ice cubes in a bar glass and add the gin and the part dry vermouth.
  Stir and then strain into a martini glass.
  Garnish with the olive on a cocktail stick.

SWEET MARTINI

Although the Dry Martini is considered the most sophisticated, the Sweet Martini has a friendly charm of its own.

- Ice cubes
- One part gin
- One part sweet vermouth
- A cocktail cherry

  Place eight ice cubes in a cocktail mixing glass.
  Add the gin and the one part sweet vermouth.
  Stir well and strain the mixture into a martini glass.
  Garnish with the cocktail cherry on a cocktail stick.

"You say alcohol is slow poison? So, who's in a hurry?"

Robert Benchley

MONTGOMERY

This is a variation of the martini. It was originally invented by Ernest Hemingway in Harry's Bar in Venice. It was during World War II and Hemingway claimed Field Marshal Montgomery would fight the enemy only if he had 15 soldiers to every one of theirs. He decided this was a good proportion of gin to vermouth.

Today, Harry's version is slightly modified and has become a speciality of the bar.

- Ten parts gin
- One part dry vermouth

- Mix the gin and part dry vermouth in a bar glass and pour into as many martini glasses as you are preparing.
- Place them in a freezer and leave until frozen solid.
- Serve frozen, so they can be sipped very slowly as they thaw.

Harry's Bar in Venice is the famed birthplace of the Montgomery cocktail.

*The Montgomery (**above left and centre**) was invented by Ernest Hemingway in honour of the famous British general of World War II. The Cardinale (**above right**) is another of Harry's famous, gin-based cocktails and could be called a martini with a difference.*

CARDINALE

This cocktail has become so popular that it can be purchased in bottled form. It is ready-mixed and available all over America and Europe.

- Six parts gin
- One part dry vermouth
- Three parts Campari
- Ice cubes

- In a bar glass, stir together the gin, vermouth and Campari with three ice cubes.
- Strain into a cocktail glass and serve ungarnished.

TOM COLLINS

Many people refer to this drink as a "John Collins" and this is understandable. The original Collins was indeed a John, the head waiter at Limmer's Hotel in London in the 18th century. He is reputed to have used the rather heavy and oily Dutch-style gin in his drink, which was not very popular in America. One barman decided to use a London brand of gin called Old Tom in the cocktail instead. The drink gained popularity instantly and became known as the Tom Collins.

- One part dry gin
- One or two dashes of sugar syrup
- The juice of one lemon
- Soda water
- Ice cubes
- A slice of lemon

Pour the gin, sugar syrup and lemon juice into a highball glass and stir it with a swizzle stick.

Top up the glass with chilled soda water, add an ice cube if required and garnish with a slice of lemon.

THE BLUE ARROW

In the normal course of events, we hardly ever eat or drink anything that is blue, so a glass of blue liquid immediately conjures up visions of something new and exciting.

- Crushed ice
- Two parts gin
- One part Cointreau
- One part lime juice cordial
- One part blue Curaçao

Place about two cups of crushed ice in a cocktail shaker.

Pour in the gin, Cointreau, lime juice and blue Curaçao and shake vigorously for about five seconds.

Strain into a chilled cocktail glass and serve ungarnished.

*Blue drinks have an exciting aura. Try the Blue Arrow (**opposite left**) and capture some of the mystery. The Tom Collins (**opposite right**) was originally made with heavy Dutch gin. Today, the lighter style of London gin is preferred.*

PINK GIN

While we are on the subject of pretty colours for drinks, let's take a look at that very English drink, Pink Gin. The famous round-the-world sailor, Sir Francis Chichester, claims that it was Pink Gins that kept him cheerful (dare we say in good spirits) during his epic voyage.

The British do it the simple way. They just shake a couple of dashes of Angostura bitters into a glass, swirl it about to coat the inside and then add a dollop of gin.

Americans tend to prefer a slightly more precise version.

- Ice cubes
- Two dashes of Angostura bitters
- Two measures of dry gin
- A twist of lemon peel (optional)

- Place four ice cubes in a bar glass and add the bitters.
- Pour in the gin, stir well and then strain into a chilled cocktail glass.
- This drink is usually served ungarnished, but you could add a twist of lemon peel for decoration if you prefer.

Joan Crawford accepts a drink from Nils Asther in Letty Lynton.

BRONX

In the days of Prohibition, each area was controlled by a different gang boss and booze played an important role in the economy of the underworld. Different areas of New York became known for the special drinks they offered. This one was the speciality of the Bronx. The secondary ingredients were probably a desperate attempt to disguise the taste of the home-made bathtub gin. Modern gin, however, turns it into an elegant treat.

- Ice cubes
- Three parts gin
- One part fresh orange juice
- One part dry vermouth

Place four or five ice cubes in a cocktail shaker. Add the three parts gin, one part fresh orange juice and the part dry vermouth and shake well.

Strain the ingredients into a cocktail glass. This elegant drink is also served ungarnished.

GIN FIZZ

This is a long, cooling drink made famous in magazine articles published as long ago as the 1870s.

- Ice cubes
- A large measure of gin
- The juice of half a lemon
- A dash of sweet gomme syrup
- One egg
- Soda water
- A slice of lemon

Place four ice cubes in a cocktail shaker and add the gin, lemon juice and gomme syrup.

Crack the egg and add the yolk or white, depending on your choice of fizz, to the shaker.

Shake vigorously for 30 seconds and strain it into a highball glass.

Top it up with chilled soda water and garnish with a slice of lemon.

*The Singapore Sling (**opposite left**) was first served in Raffles Hotel in Singapore in 1915. The addition of the white of an egg to a Gin Fizz (**opposite right**) gives it a silver fizz; the yolk would make it golden.*

SINGAPORE SLING

This cocktail became a firm favourite of writers such as Joseph Conrad and Somerset Maugham. It was an elaborate concoction designed to please female drinkers, but was soon modified and enjoyed by cocktail lovers of both sexes.

Here's a simplified and more practical version of the original Singapore Sling, which contained no less than eight ingredients.

- Ice cubes
- Two parts dry gin
- One part cherry brandy
- One part fresh lemon juice
- Soda water
- A slice of lemon
- A maraschino cherry

Place four ice cubes in a cocktail shaker and add the gin, cherry brandy and lemon juice.

Shake well and strain into a highball glass.

Top up with soda water and garnish with the slice of lemon and the maraschino cherry on a cocktail stick.

MAIDEN'S PRAYER

Oranges and lemons are traditionally associated with purity and innocence, which is why orange blossoms are often used as wedding cake decoration. Maybe this is part of the reason for this drink's name.

- Ice cubes
- One part gin
- One part Cointreau
- Half a part orange juice
- Half a part lemon juice

- Place three or four ice cubes in a cocktail shaker and add the gin, Cointreau, orange juice and lemon juice.
- Shake well and strain into a cocktail glass.

"Candy is dandy but liquor is quicker."

Ogden Nash

GIN AND TONIC

In the far-flung outposts of the British Empire, malaria was a constant danger and quinine was often used as an antidote. It didn't take Her Majesty's servants very long to discover that quinine tonic, flavoured with a dash of gin, made an incredibly fine sundowner.

- Ice cubes
- A generous measure of dry gin
- Tonic water
- A slice of lemon

- Place three ice cubes in a tall glass. Splash in a liberal measure of gin and top up the glass with the tonic water.
- Drop in a slice of lemon, twisted to release some of the zest.
- Stir gently before serving.

GIMLET

A gimlet is a small, sharp spike used for drilling holes, usually twisted into wood to make a pilot hole for a screw. When you think about it, gimlet is an appropriate name for a small, sharp drink with a twist to it.

- Ice cubes
- Two parts gin
- One part lime juice cordial
- A twist of lime rind

- Place two or three ice cubes in a cocktail mixing glass. Add the gin and lime juice cordial and stir well.
- Strain over ice cubes in a lowball glass and garnish with the twist of lime.

*Gin and Tonic (**opposite left**) has been a favourite drink wherever the British forces have raised the imperial flag. The Gimlet (**opposite right**) is one of the true classics of the cocktail world and there are about as many individual versions as there are of the equally famous martini.*

FRENCH 75

Many different cocktails were created to celebrate all kinds of events and commemorate all sorts of things. In World War 1 the French light field gun, known as the '75', was regarded as one of the world's most formidable weapons. After the War, when veterans gathered in Harry's New York Bar in Paris, a special cocktail was devised to remember the fierce field gun.

- One part chilled London dry gin
- Two dashes of sweet gomme syrup
- Chilled dry champagne
- A twist of lemon

In a champagne flute or cocktail glass, pour a measure of gin and add the two dashes of sweet gomme syrup.

Top up with champagne.

Garnish with the twist of lemon.

THE WEDDING BELLE

A pretty cocktail with which to toast the bride.

- Crushed ice
- One part gin
- One part Dubonnet rouge
- Half a part cherry brandy
- One part fresh orange juice

- Place two tablespoons of crushed ice in a cocktail shaker, add the gin, Dubonnet, cherry brandy and orange juice and shake well.
- Strain into a cocktail glass and you are ready to serve.

CHIHUAHUA BITE

Like the famous miniature Mexican dog, this drink may be petite but it certainly is lively.

- Ice cubes
- Three parts London dry gin
- One part Calvados
- One part lime juice cordial
- A twist of lemon rind

- Place three ice cubes in a cocktail shaker and add the gin, Calvados and lime juice cordial.
- Shake well and strain into a cocktail glass.
- Twist the lemon rind over it and drop it into the glass as garnish.

"I never drink anything stronger than gin before breakfast."

W. C. Fields

The Wedding Belle (opposite front) was originally made to toast a pretty bride. The Chihuahua Bite (opposite back) is an aptly named, fierce little drink.

RUM

Rum is a rich and fragrant spirit distilled from molasses in a pot still or patent still. Because molasses is produced from sugar cane (usually grown in tropical climates), the drink has become associated with the tropics, islands and beaches.

As with most distilled spirits, **rum** is clear, but is matured in oak casks and often coloured with caramel before bottling. Jamaican **rum** is usually dark, Cuban comes in light, gold or dark, while Puerto Rican **rum** is left clear. A smooth and velvety **rum** is made in the Dominican Republic and some fine **rum**s are produced in Haiti, Barbados, Antigua, Trinidad and Venezuela.

For many years **rum** formed part of the rations of sailors in the British Royal Navy. Their Pussers **Rum** (derived from the word "purser"), made in the British Virgin Islands, was issued as standard navy ration for three centuries. Dangerous jobs often called for an extra ration of **rum** to give them the necessary courage.

In a rough storm one of the worst things that could happen was that the brace controlling the mainsail yard would break under stress. Sailors would then have to go aloft, secure the two flogging ends of the broken mainbrace and splice the ends together.

This hazardous task called for a stiff draught of courage and gave rise to the expression: "Splice the mainbrace."

Drinkers have discovered that the rich **rum** taste combines perfectly with fruit juice to give a tropical flavour to cocktails, and there are hundreds of **rum**-based cocktail recipes are available to enthusiastic mixologists.

DAIQUIRI

Man is a creative animal and can adapt to almost any circumstances.

American engineers working in Daiquiri, Cuba, were upset to discover they could not obtain their usual drink, bourbon, there. But there was rum in plentiful supply, so they set about creating a drink to replace their favourite tipple.

The daiquiri was born. As with most famous cocktails, there are many versions of the daiquiri, but this simple one should serve as a starting point for the creative cocktail artist.

- Ice cubes
- One part light rum (traditionally Cuban, of course)
- The juice of half a lime
- Half a teaspoon of sugar
- A slice of lime
- A cocktail cherry

Place four or five ice cubes in a cocktail shaker. Add the rum, lime juice and sugar.

Shake very thoroughly, then strain it into a cocktail glass.

Decorate with a slice of lime and the cocktail cherry spiked on a stick.

BRASS MONKEY

In the days of sailing ship warfare, the rack on which cannon balls were stored was known as "brass monkey".

In very cold weather, the brass would contract and the cannon balls would no longer fit and pop out. Hence the expression: "Cold enough to freeze the balls off a brass monkey."

This cocktail is a good warmer when the temperature reaches brass monkey levels.

- Ice cubes
- One part light rum
- One part vodka
- Four parts orange juice
- A slice of orange

Fill a highball glass with ice cubes and pour the rum, vodka and orange juice over them.

Stir carefully and serve decorated with the slice of orange and a pretty straw.

*Ernest Hemingway always ordered double Daiquiris (**opposite left**) at La Floradita Bar in Havana, Cuba. The Brass Monkey (**opposite right**) originated in the navy.*

DAIQUIRI BLOSSOM

Not everybody enjoys the sharp astringency of the daiquiri described on the previous page. Maybe it was fine for homesick mining engineers, but in the comfort of your own home or a cosy cocktail bar you may prefer this sweeter version. It certainly has a tropical flavour to it.

- Ice cubes
- One part light rum
- One part freshly squeezed orange juice
- A dash of maraschino
- A slice of orange
- A cocktail cherry

- Place four or five ice cubes in a cocktail shaker. Add the rum, freshly squeezed orange juice and dash of maraschino.
- Shake well and strain into a cocktail glass.
- Decorate with a thin slice of orange and the cherry speared together on a cocktail stick.

BANANA DAIQUIRI

In his popular Discworld novels, author Terry Pratchett writes about an orang-utan who is inordinately fond of banana daiquiris. Readers all over the world send Pratchett recipes for this now-famous drink. This one is from a South African fan.

- Two parts light rum
- One part banana liqueur
- One part fresh lime juice
- Half a medium-sized banana
- Crushed ice
- A slice of kiwi fruit

- Place the rum, liqueur, lime juice and banana in a blender and blend for about 10 seconds until smooth and creamy.
- Add two generous scoops of crushed ice and blend for a further second or two, just to chill the drink.
- Strain into a goblet, garnish with the slice of kiwi fruit (or a slice of banana in an emergency) and serve with a straw.

FROZEN PINEAPPLE DAIQUIRI

Of course, you can go all the way with the tropical drink theme and make this rather exotic version of the famous drink. It looks good and tastes great!

- One part light rum (naturally)
- Juice of half a lime
- Two teaspoons of Cointreau
- Two slices of ripe pineapple, cut into cubes
- Crushed ice
- A cocktail cherry

- Place the rum, lime juice, Cointreau and pineapple cubes in a blender and give them a whizz until the mixture is smooth and frothy.
- Half-fill a champagne flute with crushed ice and pour the mixture over it.
- Decorate with a final cube of pineapple and the cherry spiked together on a cocktail stick.

*The Daiquiri, like the Martini, comes in many guises – Banana Daiquiri (**opposite left**), Daiquiri Blossom (**opposite centre**) and Frozen Pineapple Daiquiri (**opposite right**).*

"It's no time for mirth and laughter, The cold grey dawn of the morning after."

George Ade

THE BEE'S KISS

It's definitely not hard to guess how this sweet delight got its name. As with any bee, however, too much familiarity could produce quite a nasty sting.

- Crushed ice
- Two parts light rum

- One part clear honey
- One part thick cream

- Place about a cup of crushed ice in a cocktail shaker and pour the rum, honey and cream over it.
- Shake vigorously until blended.
- Strain into a chilled cocktail glass and serve ungarnished.

BETWEEN THE SHEETS

The perfect end to a long day is to slip in between the sheets – crisp, clean and comforting. Perhaps the inventor of this cocktail felt all those attributes had been captured in the glass.

- Ice cubes
- One part light rum
- One part brandy
- One part Cointreau
- A teaspoon of lemon juice
- A twist of lemon rind

- Place five or six ice cubes in a cocktail shaker. Add the rum, brandy, Cointreau and the teaspoon of lemon juice.
- Shake well and strain into a cocktail glass.
- Serve garnished with a twist of lemon rind.

HENRY MORGAN'S GROG

Grog was the name given to the mixture of equal parts of rum and water served to sailors in the British Royal Navy (as decreed by a naval officer nicknamed "Old Grog" after the grogram jackets he liked to wear at sea). Captain Morgan's version of grog is rather different and far more powerful.

- Crushed ice
- One part dark Jamaican rum
- Two parts Pernod
- Two parts whisky
- One part thick cream
- Ground nutmeg

- Place a scoop of crushed ice in a blender or cocktail shaker and add the rum, Pernod, whisky and cream.
- Blend or shake briskly until well mixed, and then strain it into a lowball glass.
- Dust ground nutmeg over it before serving.

APRICOT PIE

This is a fresh little cocktail for summer drinking. It's tangy and fruity and absolutely guaranteed to have you coming back for more.

- Crushed ice
- One part light rum
- One part sweet vermouth
- One teaspoon apricot brandy or to taste
- One teaspoon fresh lemon juice or to taste
- One teaspoon grenadine or to taste
- Orange peel to garnish

- Place a generous scoop of crushed ice in a cocktail shaker or a blender and add the rum, sweet vermouth, apricot brandy, lemon juice and grenadine.
- Shake or blend well and strain into a chilled cocktail glass.
- Twist the orange peel over the drink to release the zest, then drop it in as decoration.

Henry Morgan's Grog (**opposite back**) *is a pirate version of grog, it comprises equal quantities of rum and water. Apricot Pie* (**opposite front**) *makes a refreshing drink on a hot summer day.*

TOM AND JERRY

This classic cocktail is not actually named after the famous cartoon cat and mouse duo. It was invented way back in the 1850s by one Jerry Thomas, called "the professor", in his famous Planter's House bar in St Louis, Missouri. Later the name just naturally changed from Jerry Thomas to Tom and Jerry.

- One egg
- Half a part sugar syrup (or less to taste)
- One part dark Jamaican rum
- One part cognac
- Boiling water
- Grated nutmeg

Separate the yolk of the egg from the white and beat each separately. Fold them together and add the sugar syrup.

Place this mixture in a warmed coffee mug, add the rum and cognac and top up with boiling water.

Sprinkle grated nutmeg on top and serve piping hot.

THE ZOMBIE

A zombie is a corpse that has been brought back to life. Maybe the name of this cocktail refers to its restorative powers.

- Ice cubes
- One part dark rum
- One part light rum
- One part apricot brandy
- One part fresh pineapple juice
- A squeeze of lemon juice
- A squeeze of orange juice
- A slice of pineapple
- A cherry to garnish

Place four ice cubes in a cocktail shaker and add the dark and light rum, brandy, pineapple juice and the two squeezes of citrus juice.

Shake well and strain into a wine goblet.

Garnish with a slice of pineapple and a cherry threaded together on a cocktail stick.

The Zombie (**opposite front**) *and Tom and Jerry* (**opposite back**) *are two rum-based cocktails reputed to cure the common cold – or two ways to help you forget its misery!*

CUBA LIBRE

This classic cocktail is reputed to have been invented by an army officer in Cuba shortly after Coca-Cola was first produced back in the 1890s.

- Crushed ice
- One generous part light rum
- The juice of a lime
- Cola
- A slice of lime

- In a highball glass, place a small scoop of crushed ice and pour in the rum and lime juice.
- Top up with Cola and garnish with a thin wedge of fresh lime.
- It is usually served with a swizzle stick or stirrer.

Alexander Kirkland offers Irene Ward an olive in Humanity.

THE TALL ISLANDER

The name refers to the length of the drink, rather than its creator. It's a long and cooling drink and has a distinctly tropical flavour.

- Ice cubes
- One part light rum
- A dash of dark Jamaican rum
- One part pineapple juice
- A dash of lime juice
- One teaspoon sugar syrup
- Chilled soda water
- A slice of lime

- Place four ice cubes in a cocktail shaker and add the light and dark rum, part pineapple juice, dash of lime juice and the teaspoon sugar syrup.
- Shake well and strain into a highball glass.
- Add a splash of chilled soda water and several ice cubes.
- Garnish with the slice of lime.

*The Devil's Tail (**above front**) is a fiery little drink that could well be served as a "tail end" to an evening meal. In parts of Britian and America Hot Buttered Rum (**above back**) is as popular as Glühwein or the Tom and Jerry as a winter tradition.*

THE DEVIL'S TAIL

Only the very brave can catch the devil by his tail, but those who do are safe from his horns. This is definitely a drink for the bold in spirit.

- Crushed ice
- Three parts light rum
- One part vodka
- One part apricot liqueur
- One part lime juice
- A dash of grenadine
- Lime peel

Place a scoop of crushed ice in a shaker or blender. Add the rum, vodka, liqueur, lime juice (preferably fresh) and grenadine.

Shake or blend well and strain into a lowball glass.

Twist the lime peel over the glass and drop it into the drink.

HOT BUTTERED RUM

No collection of rum drinks would be complete without at least one recipe for hot buttered rum. It's a warm, sustaining drink to serve on a freezing winter's night by a roaring log fire. Buttered rum is mentioned by Charles Dickens in his book Hard Times. "Take a glass of scalding rum and butter before you get into bed," Bounderby says to Mrs Sparsit.

- The peel of a lemon or orange
- Whole cloves
- One tablespoon of brown sugar
- A cinnamon stick
- A liberal helping of dark Jamaican rum
- Half as much crème de cacao
- A pat of unsalted butter
- Grated nutmeg

Warm a large coffee mug by filling it with boiling water and letting it stand for a minute. While it is warming, take the citrus peel and stud it with as many whole cloves as you can.

Empty the coffee mug and place the studded peel in it, together with the brown sugar and cinnamon stick. Add a little boiling water and stir until the sugar has dissolved.

Add the rum, crème de cacao and fill the mug with hot water.

Remove the cinnamon stick. Drop in the butter, stir and sprinkle with grated nutmeg.

FLUFFY DUCK

It's interesting how many of the cocktails containing cream are named after animals or birds. We have the burro, the pink squirrel and the grasshopper. Now meet the duck.

- One part light rum
- One part advocaat
- Chilled lemonade
- Half a part thin cream
- A fresh strawberry and a sprig of mint

- Pour the Bacardi and advocaat into a highball glass and fill almost to the top with well-chilled lemonade.
- Trickle the cream onto the surface over the back of a spoon and garnish with the strawberry and sprig of mint.

El Burro is heavily loaded with all sorts of flavours and probably gets its name (the donkey) from the fact that it has quite a kick to it.

EL BURRO

This delightful drink should definitely be drunk in moderation if you don't want to make an ass of yourself!

- Crushed ice
- One part Kahlua
- One and a half parts dark rum
- One and a half parts coconut cream
- Two parts thin cream
- Half a banana
- Sprig of fresh mint
- Slices of banana

- Place two spoonfuls of crushed ice in a blender and add all the other ingredients, except the mint and the slices of banana.
- Blend at high speed for about 10 seconds.
- Strain into a large goblet and garnish with the slices of banana and sprig of mint.

XALAPA PUNCH

This cocktail probably originated from Xalapa, a cathedral town situated in the province of Vera Cruz in Mexico.

Here again, the size of your measure will be determined by the size of your punch bowl. In these informal times almost any large bowl will do. I have even seen punch served in a brass-bound wooden bucket. It looked great!

- The zest of two large oranges, grated
- Two parts strong black tea
- Honey or sugar to taste (about a cupful)
- One part golden rum
- One part Calvados
- One part red wine
- A block of ice
- Orange and lemon slices

- Place the grated orange zest in a saucepan and pour the hot tea over it to absorb the flavour. Leave it to cool and add the honey (or sugar if preferred). Stir until dissolved.
- Add the rum, Calvados and red wine and place in the fridge to chill.
- When ready to serve, place the block of ice in the punch bowl, pour the punch over it and garnish it with slices of orange and lemon.

ZOMBIE PUNCH

There is something a little mysterious about the idea of a zombie, and this drink certainly has a murky and mysterious look to match its name. The flavour, however, is full of life.

- Two parts light Puerto Rican rum
- One part dark Jamaican rum
- One part dark Demerara rum
- One part Triple Sec
- One part fresh lime juice
- One part fresh orange juice
- A quarter part lemon juice
- A quarter part papaya juice
- A quarter part pineapple juice
- A splash of Pernod
- A large chunk of ice
- Pineapple slices

Mix all the liquid ingredients together in a large punch bowl, then place the ice in the centre and allow it to stand for a few hours to chill.

Before the guests arrive, taste it and then adjust the flavour by adding the appropriate fruit juices or spirits.

Garnish with slices of pineapple shortly before serving.

VODKA

The word **"vodka"** comes from the Russian *Zhiznennia voda*, which means water of life. **Vodka**, or wodka (meaning "little water") is a pure spirit and can be distilled from a number of sources, including potatoes and sugar cane. The spirit is then filtered through charcoal to remove any oils or traces of impurities, and the resultant liquor is the perfect base for a cocktail. It adds the kick of alcohol without altering the flavour of the drink. Add **vodka** to lemonade and, voilà! you have alcoholic lemonade.

Vodka became popular in America in about 1946, when wartime rationing had created all kinds of shortages and drinkers grabbed whatever was available. Smirnoff **vodka** had been around as a rather unusual drink for some time, but nobody took it seriously until it was all they could get.

Typical of the popular **vodka**-based drinks is the Screwdriver, which consists of **vodka** and orange juice and is said to have been invented by construction workers who wanted to add excitement to their lunchtime drink of orange juice. A dash of **vodka** made the difference, and a quick stir with a handy screwdriver got it properly mixed into the juice.

Vodka is the ideal drink for the beginner bar-tender to use in experiments. Whatever new flavour of mixer comes onto the market, you just add **vodka** and you've invented a new cocktail. Ideally, **vodka** should be stored in the freezer and served almost painfully cold. Purists like to drink it neat, tossing back a small glass in a single gulp.

THE Q MARTINI

The James Bond series of books and films has spawned a number of popular drinks, including this intriguing blue version of the Martini.

- Ice cubes
- Two parts vodka
- A splash of blue Curaçao
- Half a part lime juice
- A twist of lemon rind

Place three ice cubes in a cocktail bar glass. Add the vodka, blue Curaçao and lime juice.

Stir until well blended and strain into a cocktail glass.

Serve decorated with a twist of lemon rind.

BLOODY MARY

Today the Bloody Mary is probably the most popular vodka-based cocktail in the world and there are many variations of this tempting drink.

But it must have taken some courage to create the first one. It needs imagination to blend two such disparate drinks as fiery, crystal-clear vodka and thick, slightly lumpy tomato juice. But there's no doubt it works, whatever way you make it. Here's a starter recipe.

- Ice cubes
- Two parts vodka
- Six parts tomato juice
- A teaspoon of tomato sauce (catsup)
- A dash of Worcestershire sauce
- A dash of Tabasco sauce
- A pinch of celery salt
- A stick of celery
- A dusting of finely ground white pepper

Place four ice cubes in a cocktail shaker and add the vodka and tomato juice.

Add the tomato sauce, Worcestershire sauce, Tabasco sauce and celery salt.

Shake well and strain into a highball glass.

Decorate with a stick of celery.

Finish with a light dusting of white pepper. (You could use black pepper instead, but it looks very unappetising, rather like cigar ash that has been sprinkled on the surface of the drink.)

*Another vodka-based cocktail, the Q Martini (**above left**) has the added attraction of being blue. Legend has it that the barman of Harry's New York Bar in Paris named the Bloody Mary (**above right**) after the glamorous Hollywood actress, Mary Pickford.*

VODKATINI

It's interesting to see what factors influence the popularity of a cocktail. The vodka martini must be one of the best-known cocktails in the world today, just because the famous and fictitious James Bond, 007, has been drinking vodka martinis for the past 36 years.

- Ice cubes
- Two parts vodka (preferably from Russia)
- One part dry vermouth
- A twist of lemon rind

"*A woman drove me to drink and I didn't even have the courtesy to thank her.*"

W. C. Fields

- Place about five ice cubes in a bar glass, add the vodka and vermouth and stir well.
- Strain the mixture into a cocktail glass and decorate it with a twist of lemon rind.

RUSSIAN COFFEE

The Russians have the reputation not only of making the best vodka but of being able to drink it in large quantities. And who needs ordinary coffee when there's a drink as warming as this one to keep out the Siberian chill? Names and styles vary from bartender to bartender.

- One part vodka
- One part coffee liqueur (Tia Maria or Kahlua)
- One part thin cream
- Half a cup of crushed ice
- Cocoa powder (optional)

- Place all the ingredients in a blender and give them a brisk whirl for about 10 seconds.
- Pour the result into a chilled champagne saucer and decorate with a swirl of cream.
- You could also sprinkle a dusting of cocoa powder on the surface for added flavour.

BLUE LAGOON

The Blue Lagoon is a cooling, ice blue summer drink. There's always something a little special about serving a blue drink.

- Crushed ice
- Three parts vodka
- One part blue Curaçao
- Three parts pineapple juice
- Three dashes of green chartreuse
- A slice of pineapple
- A cocktail cherry (optional)

- Place half a cup of crushed ice in a cocktail shaker and add the vodka, Curaçao, pineapple juice and green chartreuse.
- Shake well and strain into a low-ball glass.
- Serve the drink decorated with a slice of pineapple, and a cocktail cherry if you feel like adding even more colour.

Add a touch of mystery to a cocktail party with a Blue Lagoon (**opposite left**). *The Black Cossack* (**opposite right**) *is a stunningly simple combination of vodka and Guinness stout.*

BLACK COSSACK

Why anybody should want to mess with Guinness, goodness knows. But this is a simple drink and popular in some parts.

- A large slug of vodka
- A glass of Guinness stout

- Simply pour the vodka very carefully into the stout and drink it.
Don't stir or shake it, as the froth would be overwhelming.

Robert Montgomery (**above**) *raises his glass in* Letty Lynton.

BULLSHOT

We should not be at all surprised to find vodka teamed up with savoury flavours after the great success of the Bloody Mary. The Bullshot is reputed to be a fine remedy for hangover blues.

- Ice cubes
- One part vodka
- Three parts chilled clear beef bouillon
- A dash of lemon juice
- A dash of Worcestershire sauce
- A pinch of celery salt
- A slice of lemon

- Place five or six ice cubes in a bar glass and add the vodka and beef bouillon.
- Add the lemon juice, Worcestershire sauce and celery salt.
- Stir well and strain over ice cubes in a lowball glass.
- Serve garnished with a lemon slice.

HARVEY WALLBANGER

The story behind the intriguing name of this drink is that Harvey was a surfer who was eliminated in a surfing championship in California. He was so angry at his defeat that he headed for Pancho's Bar at Manhattan Beach and soothed his bruised ego by drinking a large quantity of vodka and Galliano. He then banged his head against a wall and urged his friends to take him home and stop his destructive drinking.

Whether it's true or not, the name has stuck and the drink is a firm favourite throughout the world.

- Ice cubes
- Two parts vodka
- Five parts fresh orange juice
- One part Galliano
- A slice of orange

Place four or five ice cubes in a cocktail shaker and add the vodka and orange juice.

Shake well and strain into a highball glass.

Add two ice cubes and gently float the Galliano on top.

Garnish with a slice of orange on the rim of the glass and serve with a straw.

MOSCOW MULE

You can now purchase ready-mixed Moscow Mules in cans, but it's far more fun to make your own, complete with your own variations and personal touches. When it comes to cocktails, creativity is the name of the game.

- Ice cubes
- One generous part vodka
- A teaspoon of lime juice
- Ginger beer
- A slice of fresh lime

Place two ice cubes in a chilled highball glass and pour in the vodka and lime juice.

Stir thoroughly and fill with ginger beer.

Garnish with the slice of lime and serve.

THE VOLGA BOATMAN

I doubt whether any Volga boatman could have afforded this drink, unless his boat happened to be an elegant pleasure craft.

- Crushed ice
- One part vodka
- One part cherry brandy
- One part fresh orange juice
- A maraschino cherry

Place three spoons of crushed ice in a cocktail shaker, add the vodka, cherry brandy and orange juice.

Shake well and strain into a cocktail glass.

Garnish with the cherry on a cocktail stick and serve.

"You're not drunk if you can lie on the floor without holding on."

Dean Martin

*The Moscow Mule (**opposite left**) and Volga Boatman (**opposite right**) demonstrate how vodka teams up with any fruit flavours.*

WHITE RUSSIAN

This smooth white cocktail probably reminded its inventor of the glistening snow of Siberia. It's certainly a great comforter on a frosty night.

- Crushed ice
- One part vodka
- One part white crème de cacao
- One part thick cream

- Place two spoons of crushed ice in a cocktail shaker and add the vodka, crème de cacao and cream.
- Shake the combination well and strain into a chilled cocktail glass and serve ungarnished.

BANANA PUNCH

Here's a truly tropical drink which uses three kinds of fruit flavours to create a jungle taste.

- Crushed ice
- One part vodka
- One part apricot brandy
- The juice of half a lime
- Soda water
- A sliced banana
- A sprig of fresh mint

- Place a scoop of crushed ice in a cocktail shaker and add the vodka, apricot brandy and lime juice.
- Shake well and strain into a highball glass.
- Top up with soda water and decorate with slices of banana and the mint.

*The White Russian (**opposite left**), a rich and creamy drink for a chilly evening, and Banana Punch (**opposite right**), one of those deliciously dangerous drinks that will last you the whole evening.*

VODKA GIMLET

We often encounter the vodka equivalents of drinks that were originally made with gin. This is a typical one and, like the original Gimlet, there are many versions of this classic drink. We offer a basic version and leave it to you to create your own personal variations.

- Ice cubes
- Two parts vodka
- One part Rose's lime juice cordial
- A teaspoon of sugar syrup
- A slice of orange

- Place three ice cubes in a cocktail shaker and add the vodka, lime juice and sugar syrup.
- Shake well and strain into a cocktail glass.
- Garnish with a slice of orange.

SALVATORE

This is one of those superb cocktails that manages to combine sweet and tart flavours in exactly the right proportions (as long as you mix it right, of course).

- Ice cubes
- Two parts vodka
- One part Kirsch
- One part Cointreau
- One part fresh grapefruit juice
- A maraschino cherry

- Place four ice cubes in a cocktail shaker and add the vodka, Kirsch, Cointreau and grapefruit juice.
- Shake well and then strain into a cocktail glass.
- Serve decorated with a cherry on a cocktail stick.

Sweet and sour flavours combine happily in the Vodka Gimlet (**opposite left**) *and the tangy Salvatore* (**opposite right**).

SCOTCH FROG

I have no idea how this rather punchy drink got its name. Perhaps it is rather like Welsh rarebit, which is reputed to be the poor Welsh householder's substitute for rabbit. But why should any self-respecting Scot want a substitute for a frog?

- Ice cubes
- Two parts vodka
- One part Galliano
- One part Cointreau
- The juice of a lime
- A dash of Angostura bitters
- Maraschino cherry juice or cherry liqueur

  Place three ice cubes in a cocktail shaker and add the vodka, Galliano, Cointreau, lime juice, bitters and the cherry juice or cherry liqueur.
  Shake well and strain into a cocktail glass.
  Serve ungarnished.

The Black Marble (opposite front) has the elegant simplicity of a good dry martini. The tartness of lime is offset by the sweetness of the liqueurs in the Scotch Frog (opposite back).

"I fear the man who drinks water, as he remembers this morning what the rest of us said last night."

Greek saying

THE BLACK MARBLE

Like many of the great classics of the cocktail world, the Black Marble is uncomplicated, but very chic.

- Ice cubes
- A large black olive
- One part good Polish or Russian vodka
- A slice of orange

  Fill a lowball glass or wine goblet with ice cubes. Place the black olive right in the centre and pour the vodka over it.
  Serve garnished with a slice of fresh orange.

CHERRY VODKA

Vodka combines well with almost any fruit flavour, as this pretty cocktail demonstrates.

- Crushed ice
- Two parts chilled vodka
- One part fresh lime juice
- One part cherry liqueur
- A maraschino cherry

Place three spoons of crushed ice in a cocktail shaker, add the vodka, lime juice and cherry liqueur and shake well.

Strain the mixture into a chilled cocktail glass.

Decorate with the cherry on a cocktail stick.

THE KREMLIN COLONEL

This vodka-based creation deserves promotion to the highest rank.

- Crushed ice
- Two parts vodka
- Half a part fresh lime juice
- A teaspoon of sugar (or to taste)
- Mint leaves

- Place a spoon of ice in a cocktail shaker and add the vodka, lime juice and sugar.
- Shake well and strain into a cocktail glass.
- Tear the mint leaves to release the aroma and drop them on to the drink as garnish.

THE SOVIET

Like the cuddly Russian bear, this vodka drink is stronger than it looks.

- Crushed ice
- Three parts vodka
- One part sweet sherry
- One part dry vermouth
- Lemon peel

Place a scoop of crushed ice in a shaker, add the vodka, sherry and vermouth and shake well. Strain into a cocktail glass. Serve garnished with the lemon peel.

SALTY DOG

The salted rim of the glass used for this cocktail turns it into a complete taste experience.

- Ice cubes
- Four parts vodka
- One part unsweetened grapefruit juice
- One teaspoon lemon juice
- Fine salt

Place three ice cubes in a cocktail shaker and add the vodka, grapefruit juice and lemon juice and shake well.

Frost the rim of a chilled cocktail glass with fine salt and strain the cocktail into glass.

Undoubtedly Russian in origin and style, the Soviet (above left) is a punchy little drink. The Salty Dog (above right) is almost a classic and is to vodka what margarita is to tequila.

The Absolut bottle (right) is made of special translucent glass and the label is engraved rather than stuck on the bottle.

WHISKEY

Whisky (or whiskey, depending on its origin) is made in many parts of the world. The spirit produced in Scotland is probably the best known and is spelled without the "e", **whisky**. This is usually simply referred to as Scotch. All other **whiskies** are spelled with an "e" to distinguish them from the "real thing".

It should be said right away that most Scots would be horrified at the thought of their national drink being adulterated with anything at all, apart from a little water to bring out the natural flavour. Unless you are an active masochist it is not advisable to offer a **whisky**-based cocktail to a true Scot.

This is probably why almost all **whisky** and **whiskey** cocktails were developed in America and not Scotland. This being so, the chances are the original recipes calling for "**whisky**" referred to American bourbon and not Scotch.

Good **whiskey** is also made in Ireland, Canada and even in Japan, so there are many different flavours from which to choose.

Even in Scotland there are many styles and the best known are "single malts", produced from a particular distillery, while most commercially available **whiskies** are blended ones, made from the products of several regions.

Essentially, **whisky** is distilled from a fermented mash made of malted grain. In Scotland it derives much of its rich flavour from peat. The water used in **whisky**-making flows over peat beds, picking up its earthy flavour, and peat is burned to warm the sprouted grain and stop further growth. The pale blue smoke leaves its distinctive flavour in the malt.

SCOTCH OLD-FASHIONED

Here's a cocktail that adds a bittersweet touch to whisky. No doubt the Scots would disapprove strongly of any addition to what they believe is already the perfect drink, but if you're not Scottish you might like to try it.

- A cube of sugar
- A few dashes of Angostura bitters
- Two measures of Scotch whisky
- Ice cubes

- Soak a sugar cube in Angostura bitters and place it in the bottom of a lowball glass.
- Add just enough water to dissolve the sugar and then pour in the measures of whisky. Stir gently and drop in two ice cubes.

THREE RIVERS

This classic drink was invented in Canada and is often known by its French name, Trois Rivieres.

- Ice cubes
- Two parts whiskey

(preferably Canadian)
- One part Dubonnet
- One part Triple Sec

- Place four or five ice cubes in a cocktail shaker, add the whiskey, Dubonnet and Triple Sec.
- Shake well and strain into a lowball glass.
- Serve ungarnished.

MINT JULEP

This drink reeks of good living in an age when there were slaves and servants available at the flick of a finger to do the bidding of the master.

A good Mint Julep is a drink for the wealthy. Not many people today will be able to afford the "tankard of bourbon" that forms the basis of the drink. But for those occasions when you do feel like a millionaire, here's the recipe.

- Crushed ice
- A tankard of bourbon
- A teaspoon of caster sugar
- Two tablespoons of water
- A teaspoon of Barbados rum
- A large bunch of freshly picked mint

Place a cup of crushed ice in a pitcher and add the bourbon, caster sugar, water and rum. Stir well.

Crush the mint leaves lightly to release the flavour and place them in a serving jug.

Strain the contents of the bar glass into the jug, add four or five ice cubes and serve in lowball glasses.

Clockwise from top: *Mint Julep originated in the United States' Deep South in the days of the cotton barons and Mississippi steamboats. The Scotch Old-Fashioned, a classic cocktail, was created around 1900. Although probably first made with Canadian whiskey, Three Rivers tastes just as good made with any good whisky.*

THE WALDORF COCKTAIL

By using different blends of whiskey you can create a whole range of different Waldorf cocktails. Traditionally, bourbon is used.

- Crushed ice
- Two parts bourbon
- One part Pernod
- One part sweet vermouth
- A dash of Angostura bitters

Place a scoop of crushed ice in a bar glass and add the bourbon, Pernod, sweet vermouth and Angostura bitters.

Stir well and strain into a chilled cocktail glass.

ROB ROY

This drink was named after the famous Scottish hero and should be poured whenever a toast is drunk to heroes.

- Ice cubes
- Two dashes of Angostura bitters
- One generous part Scotch whisky
- One equally generous part sweet vermouth
- A twist of orange

Place two ice cubes in a lowball glass and splash in two dashes of bitters.

Add the whisky and vermouth, garnish with a twist of orange and serve.

"Love makes the world go round. Whisky makes it go round twice as fast."

Compton Mackenzie

LADY HUNT

An elegant and equally delicious cocktail that is tangy and crisp in character, but also gently mellow.

- Three parts malt whisky
- One part Tia Maria
- One part Amaretto
- The juice of half a lemon
- A dash of egg white
- Ice cubes
- A slice of orange
- A maraschino cherry

Place all the ingredients with the exception of the orange slice and cherry into a cocktail shaker with four ice cubes and shake briskly.

Strain into a cocktail glass and decorate with the slice of orange and the maraschino cherry.

NEW ORLEANS

Many cocktails got their names from the places where they were invented. This one obviously originated in the southern parts of the United States and evokes images of the Mardi Gras and Dixieland jazz.

- Crushed ice
- Three parts bourbon
- One part Pernod
- Three dashes of Angostura bitters
- A dash of anisette
- A teaspoon of sugar syrup (or less to taste)
- Ice cubes
- A twist of lemon

- Place a scoop of crushed ice in a cocktail shaker and add the bourbon, Pernod, bitters, anisette and sugar syrup.
- Shake vigorously and strain into a lowball glass filled with ice cubes. Garnish with a twist of lemon before serving.

SPIRIT OF SCOTLAND

This cocktail is most appropriately named, since Drambuie is made of whisky, heather and honey. What could be more Scottish?

- Crushed ice
- Two parts Scotch whisky
- One part Drambuie
- Half a part lemon juice

- Place a scoop of crushed ice in a blender or cocktail shaker and add the whisky, Drambuie and lemon juice.
- Blend everything together briskly and strain into a cocktail glass.

"Freedom and whisky gang the gither!"

Robert Burns

*New Orleans (**opposite left**) is a tangy and complex array of flavours. In Spirit of Scotland (**opposite right**), two well-known products of Scotland are combined.*

SAZERAC

This romantic drink derived its name from the company importing brandy from France, Sazerac du Forge et Fils. Later, rye whiskey replaced the brandy in the recipe, but the name remained the same.

- A lump of sugar
- A dash of Angostura bitters
- Ice cubes
- Two generous parts of rye whiskey
- A dash of Pernod
- A twist of lemon

SCOTCH MIST

The simplest version of Scotch Mist is simply Scotch on the rocks with a twist of lemon zest over it. This hot version is served in a tea cup and is known, for some strange reason, as the "English" Scotch mist. It's probably something to do with the tea.

- One part Scotch whisky
- Three parts freshly brewed Ceylon tea
- Honey to taste
- Thick cream

- Mix the whisky and tea together and add the honey to taste, stirring over a low heat until almost (but not quite) boiling.
- Pour into small (demitasse) coffee cups and float a teaspoon of cream onto the surface of each drink.

- Soak the sugar lump in Angostura bitters and place it in a cooled lowball glass with an ice cube.
- Add the whiskey and stir well. Add the Pernod and twist the lemon rind over the glass.

*This version of Scotch Mist (**opposite left**) is also called English Scotch Mist and served hot. The Sazerac (**opposite right**) is a rather romantic drink that originated in New Orleans.*

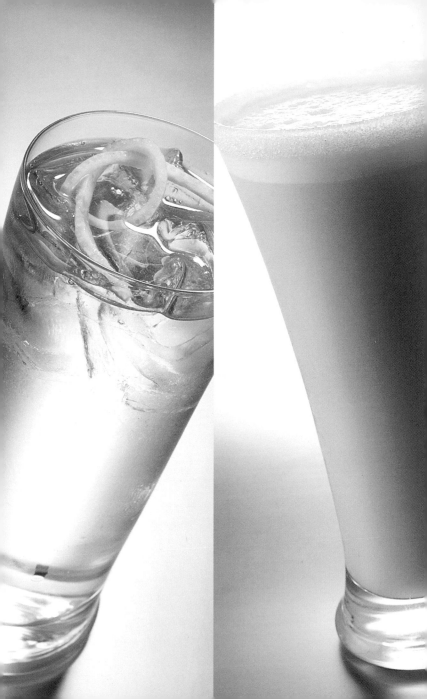

LEPRECHAUN

It is said that if you capture a leprechaun he will grant you a wish, but who could wish for more than this merry wee drink?

- Ice cubes
- One part Irish whiskey (a large one, of course)
- Two parts tonic water
- Lemon peel

- Place two ice cubes in a highball glass and add the whiskey and tonic.
- Stir reverently and twist the lemon peel over it. Drop in the twisted peel and serve.

EVERYTHING BUT

Now here's a truly dangerous drink. Apart from the alcohol, it also has other exciting ingredients, such as caster sugar, citrus and a whole egg, that only go into the most daring drinks.

No wonder it's called Everything But – the missing words are probably "the Kitchen Sink".

It's actually more of a joke drink than a serious one. When you ask a guest what he wants and he says, "Everything", this is it. Here goes.

- Ice cubes
- One part rye whiskey
- One part dry gin
- One part lemon juice
- One part orange juice
- One egg
- Half a part apricot brandy
- One teaspoon of caster sugar

- Place six ice cubes in a cocktail shaker and add the whiskey, gin, lemon and orange juice, the egg, apricot brandy and caster sugar to taste.
- Shake very well until smooth and velvety and strain into a highball glass. You may add ice cubes if required.
- If you really want to go the whole hog, frost the rim of the glass with caster sugar before pouring the drink.

*The Leprechaun (**opposite left**) is a merry little Irish drink which calls for a good measure of fine Irish whiskey. Everything But (**opposite right**) combines three of the most popular (and very alcoholic) cocktail spirits – gin, whiskey and apricot brandy – all in one power-packed drink.*

THE BOILERMAKER

It could be argued that this rough-and-ready drink is not a cocktail, as it is taken in two parts. It certainly is a mixed drink, though. I've seen it drunk in several countries, by drinkers in various stages of alcoholic merriment.

- A shot glass of blended whisky
- A mug of lager beer

The shot glass of whisky is usually swallowed in a single gulp, followed by a glass of beer. Sometimes the whisky and beer are mixed in a glass or tankard and drunk together.

COMFORTABLE SCREW

Southern Comfort is an orange-and-peach-flavoured whiskey produced in the southern United States.

- Ice cubes
- One part Southern Comfort
- Six parts fresh orange juice
- A banana

  Place six ice cubes in a cocktail shaker and add the Southern Comfort and orange juice.
  Shake well and strain into a low-ball glass.
  Garnish with the banana and serve.

CLUBMAN COCKTAIL

Irish Mist is a liqueur based on Irish whiskey flavoured with herbs and honey and produced in Tulach Mhor, Ireland. The Clubman is a very colourful drink, guaranteed to start the conversation flowing.

- Ice cubes
- One part Irish Mist
- Four parts orange juice

- A dessertspoon of egg white
- A dash of blue Curaçao

  Place four ice cubes in a cocktail shaker and add the Irish Mist, orange juice and egg white.

- Shake briskly and strain into a lowball glass.
- Carefully trickle the blue Curaçao down the sides of the glass (you might like to use a straw) to create a marbled effect.

*The Comfortable Screw (**front**) gets its name from the fact that it is a Screwdriver made with Southern Comfort instead of vodka. In the Clubman Cocktail (**back**), blue Curaçao is trickled down the sides of the glass to create the blue veins.*

DOM PEDRO

This has become a firm favourite in South Africa and appears there on many restaurant menus. The strange thing about it is that nobody seems to know who Dom Pedro was or how this sweet delight got its name. There are two basic versions, one using whisky and the other using Kahlua.

- Vanilla ice cream
- A generous measure of whisky or Kahlua
- Chocolate vermicelli

- Fill a lowball glass or goblet with soft vanilla ice cream and pour the whisky or Kahlua over it.
- Whip briskly with a fork until well blended and serve garnished with a sprinkling of chocolate vermicelli. It is usual to provide a long bar spoon to help reach the bottom bits.

*Dom Pedro (***opposite left***), a stunningly simple combination of ice cream and whisky. Irish Coffee (***opposite right***) was originally created by the bartender at Shannon Airport near the Irish coast in the late 1940s.*

IRISH COFFEE

This is a fine alternative to ordinary coffee at the end of a good meal. The Irish have long been putting a dash of whiskey in their tea and calling it Irish tea, but the barman changed the recipe slightly to appeal to the American airmen who were using Shannon Airport as their base during World War II. Americans have always preferred coffee to tea.

You can actually buy an Irish liqueur called Irish Velvet, which is based on Irish whiskey, black coffee and sugar. It's not as pleasant, or as much fun, as making your own.

- One part Irish whiskey
- Five parts strong, black coffee
- A teaspoon of brown sugar
- One part thick cream

- Pour the Irish whiskey and hot coffee into a warmed Irish coffee glass, which is sometimes a goblet with a handle like a teacup and sometimes shaped like a large wineglass.
- Add brown sugar to taste and stir gently until it is dissolved.
- Trickle the cream over the back of a teaspoon onto the surface of the coffee.

WHITE HEATHER

Bartenders throughout the world compete regularly at international gatherings, where new drinks are tried, discussed and judged. This award-winning recipe, invented by barman Rodney Brock, specified the brand of each of the ingredients, but we leave it to readers to select their own. It really is a wonderful drink.

- Ice cubes
- One part Scotch whisky
- One part crème de banane
- One part crème de cacao
- Two parts thin cream
- Nutmeg

Place three ice cubes in a cocktail shaker and add all the other ingredients except the nutmeg.

Shake well and strain into a cocktail glass.

Grate nutmeg over the drink and serve.

RATTLESNAKE

One of the many slang names for illicit moonshine liquor was "snake juice", which probably referred to the rough mountain-distilled spirit. This is a refined version, using bourbon.

- Crushed ice
- Two parts bourbon
- One teaspoon of lemon juice
- One teaspoon of sugar syrup
- Half an egg white
- Several dashes of Pernod

Place a scoop of crushed ice in a cocktail shaker and add the bourbon, lemon juice, sugar syrup, egg white and Pernod.

Shake vigorously for 10 seconds or more and strain it into a chilled lowball glass.

The White Heather (**opposite left**) *won an award in Hamburg, Germany, in 1984. The egg white added to the Rattlesnake* (**opposite right**) *gives it its silky texture.*

CHAMPAGNE AND WINE

Purists will be horrified at the thought of adding anything to **wine**. Even an ice cube in a glass of Chardonnay raises eyebrows. But we shouldn't worry too much about fanatics. **Wine**, sparkling or still, has been used in all sorts of mixtures for centuries. Like so many of life's pleasures, **wine** mixtures were often born of necessity. On freezing cold European winter evenings, a mug of steaming mulled **wine** was a real comfort. Before the discovery of the cork stopper, **wines** did not last as long as they do today. Red **wine** stored in a barrel or amphora sealed with a wooden stopper wrapped in linen would turn to vinegar after a year or so, and needed all the help it could get. A selection of warming spices did the trick, and Glühweins and Gloggs were born.

The Greeks sealed their **wine** jars with wooden stoppers and poured melted resin over them to keep out the air. Obviously some resin got into the **wine** and made retsina. Today it's almost the national drink of Greece and the resin is added deliberately, although the need for wooden stoppers is long past.

The French, who would not think of enjoying a meal without **wine**, bring up their children on watered **wine** until they are old enough to drink it neat. And if you're happy to dilute it with water, why not with something else?

Champagne has been called the king of wines, and like all good rulers, it mixes comfortably with all manner of lesser subjects. It can be combined with almost any liqueur or fruit juice to create a wide range of exciting **cocktails**, and is said to be the only **wine** that may acceptably be served at breakfast.

WINE COLLINS

As with many successful drinks, this one depends on achieving just the right balance between sweet and sour. It uses a sweet wine as a base, balancing the sweetness with the juice of a fresh lime.

- Ice cubes
- Four parts Madeira, Marsala or ruby port
- Half a part fresh lime juice
- Dry lemon drink
- A maraschino cherry

• Place four ice cubes in a mixing glass and add the wine and lime juice. Stir well and strain into a lowball glass.

• Top up with the dry lemon drink. Stir lightly to retain the sparkle and garnish with the cherry on a stick.

WALTZING MATILDA

Here's a good summer cooler.

- Crushed ice
- Four parts dry white wine
- One part gin
- One part passion fruit juice
- Half a teaspoon of Curaçao
- Soda water or ginger ale according to your taste
- Orange peel

- Place a generous scoop of crushed ice in a cocktail shaker and add the wine, gin, passion fruit juice (you could also use passion fruit cordial if the real thing is not available to you) and the Curaçao.
- Shake briskly, then strain the contents into a highball glass.
- Top up with the sparkling mixer of your choice and garnish with a twist of orange peel.

- A pinch of grated nutmeg
- Five parts red Bordeaux-style wine
- One part ruby port
- One part brandy

Place the lemon peel, cloves, cinnamon and nutmeg in a saucepan, add the liquid ingredients and heat slowly until almost, but not quite, boiling. If it is allowed to boil it loses its alcohol.

Strain the drink into a warmed coffee mug.

MULLED CLARET

Mulled wine has been a traditional winter drink for centuries. Modern recipes, compared with those of days gone by, are slightly more refined, better tasting and certainly with more of a kick.

- The peel of a lemon
- Six whole cloves
- Ground cinnamon to taste

SHERRY SHANDY

Here's a very refreshing summer drink that can be made as concentrated or as weak as you please.

- Three dashes of Angostura bitters
- Two sherry glasses of amontillado sherry
- A bottle of ginger ale or ginger beer
- Ice cubes
- A slice of lemon

Betty Compson pours John Darrow a restorative drink in The Lady Refuses.

- Splash the measure of bitters into a chilled highball glass and swirl it around to coat the inside of the glass.
- Pour in the sherry and then fill the glass with the ginger ale or ginger beer.
- Float an ice cube on the top and serve garnished with a slice of lemon.

SHERRY EGGNOG

The Sherry Eggnog is a smooth and sensual drink that has a lovely velvety texture.

- Crushed ice
- Two sherry glasses of amontillado sherry
- A dessertspoon of caster sugar (or to taste)
- A fresh egg
- A cup of milk
- Grated nutmeg

- Place half a cup of crushed ice in a blender or cocktail shaker. Add the sherry, caster sugar, egg and milk and shake or blend until the consistency is perfectly smooth and velvety.
- Strain into a chilled highball glass and dust with grated nutmeg to decorate.

SANGRIA

Sangria is one of the old traditional punches that is much enjoyed in Spanish-speaking countries. Its name is derived from the Spanish *sangre*, meaning blood, and obviously refers to its colour. There are almost as many recipes for sangria as there are for martinis. Interestingly, sangria is one of the few punches that is made as an individual drink as well as a communal cocktail. We have used large quantities here, but you can scale them down quite drastically to suit your own needs.

A nice touch is to serve the sangria in a goblet that has a sugar-frosted rim. It turns the drink into a really special occasion.

- Two bottles of red wine
- Half a cup of Curaçao
- Half a cup of brandy
- The juice of an orange
- The juice of a lemon or lime
- Half a cup of caster sugar (or to taste)
- A chunk of ice
- Orange, peach and lemon slices
- Soda water (optional)

- Mix all the liquid ingredients, except the soda water.
- Add the caster sugar and strain into a punch bowl containing a chunk of ice.
- Garnish with the fruit slices.
- Add the soda water shortly before serving.

"Drinking makes such fools of people, and people are such fools to begin with that it's compounding a felony."

Robert Benchley

CHAMPAGNE CLASSIC

There are several versions of the Champagne Classic, some of which leave out the brandy. It's a simple and deliciously elegant drink.

- A cube of sugar
- A dash of Angostura bitters
- Chilled dry champagne
- A teaspoon of brandy
- A cocktail cherry

- Place the cube of sugar in a champagne flute and add a dash or two of Angostura bitters.
- The carefully fill the glass with champagne.
- Add the teaspoon of brandy.
- Serve decorated with the cocktail cherry.

The art of sabrage – decapitating a bottle of champagne with a sabre – can still be used to start a party with a bang, but practise in private first.

BELLINI

The Bellini became the favourite drink of celebrities such as Noël Coward and Ernest Hemingway when they visited Harry's Bar in Venice. It's easy to see why.

Modern bartenders may be tempted to use the readily available canned or boxed peach juice for this drink, but the real connoisseur would never accept anything but the fresh juice of ripe peaches. It really is worth the extra effort.

Peel several ripe peaches and remove the stones. Place them in a blender and whip them into a smooth purée. In his cookbook,

Harry's Bar's present owner, Arrigo, says they never used anything as crude as a blender in the "good old days". Small white peaches were squeezed by hand and pushed through a sieve to make the pulp.

- One generous part fresh peach juice
- Four equally generous parts dry champagne
- A peach slice

Pour the fruit juice into a champagne flute, filling it about a quarter full.

Top up the glass with champagne.
Do not stir or shake.

Garnish with the peach slice on the rim of the glass and serve.

The Bellini was created in the 1940s by Guiseppe Cipriani, founder of Harry's Bar in Venice, in honour of the famous Venetian painter, Bellini.

KIR ROYALE

This drink was first named Kir after the war hero and mayor of Dijon, Felix Kir. In smart cocktail bars, the rough peasant wine was later replaced with fine champagne and the drink elevated to royal status.

Today, Kir is the same drink made with dry white wine; Kir Royale is the version that uses champagne.

- Seven parts chilled dry champagne
- One part chilled crème de cassis (or raspberry liqueur if you prefer)
- A twist of lemon rind

- Fill a champagne flute about three-quarters full with chilled champagne.
- Add liqueur and serve garnished with the twist of lemon rind.

BLACK VELVET

It is not difficult to see how this old favourite got its name. A good stout has a smooth, creamy consistency rather like liquid velvet, and the sparkling wine adds a special glow.

The drink is said to have been created in Brooks' London Club in 1861 when Queen Victoria and the rest of Britain was in mourning for Prince Albert. The barman created this solemn drink by using Guinness stout and champagne.

- One bottle or can of Guinness stout
- A bottle of dry champagne

- Half-fill the glass with the Guinness stout and then gently pour in the champagne, trying to create as little foam as possible.
- Serve without ice or garnish.

ROSSINI

Here's a pretty and very refreshing drink to serve when strawberries are in season – perfect while watching tennis at Wimbledon.

- One part puréed strawberries
- Three parts dry sparkling wine
- One fresh strawberry

- Pour the strawberry purée into a champagne flute and top up with chilled sparkling wine. Stir very gently, trying not to dissipate the bubbles.
- Float the fresh strawberry on top and serve.

DEATH IN THE AFTERNOON

Like many of the champagne-based cocktails, it requires very gentle handling to retain the delicate bubbles.

- Ice cubes
- One part Pernod
- Chilled dry champagne

- Place two ice cubes in the bottom of a champagne flute and add the Pernod.
- Slowly pour in champagne to fill the glass and stir very gently so as not to lose the sparkle.
- Serve ungarnished.

"Indeed, indeed, repentance oft before I swore – but was I sober when I swore?"

Omar Khayyam

*The Rossini (**opposite right**), a variation of the Bellini, uses fresh strawberry purée instead of peach juice. Death in the Afternoon (**opposite left**) is said to have been a favourite of Ernest Hemingway when he lived in Paris.*

CHAMPAGNE BLUES

This dramatic drink was created by barman and author John J. Poister as a tribute to the authors of Champagne Blues, Nan and Ivan Lyons. They say it's impossible to have the blues when you're drinking champagne, so maybe we should take note of this as a remedy for depression.

- Dry champagne
- Blue Curaçao
- Lemon peel

- Pour the chilled champagne into a chilled tulip glass and add the blue Curaçao to taste.
- Twist the lemon peel over the drink to release the zest and drop it into the glass as a garnish. Cheer up.

PRINCE OF WALES

Here is another champagne-based drink with a royal connection. It was probably a firm favourite of Queen Victoria's son, Alfred, who seems to have led a merry life as he toured about the British Empire.

- Ice cubes
- One part brandy
- One part Madeira or any sweet, fortified white wine
- Three drops of Curaçao
- Two dashes of Angostura bitters
- Chilled dry champagne
- A slice of orange

- Place five ice cubes in a cocktail shaker and add the brandy, sweet wine, Curaçao and Angostura bitters.
- Shake well and strain into a tall champagne flute. Fill it gently with champagne and garnish it with a slice of orange.

Previous pages from left to right: *Champagne Blues, Prince of Wales, Buck's Fizz and Southern Champagne, four classic champagne-based cocktails.*

BUCK'S FIZZ

Arguably the most common of all champagne-based drinks, Buck's Fizz is now served regularly at champagne breakfasts and celebrity lunches. It is is certainly invigorating and an ideal early-morning drink that can be made as strong or weak as you please. It is said to have been invented by the barman at Buck's Club in London in the 1920s. One can buy Buck's Fizz ready-mixed in a bottle or can, but it will never replace the real thing.

- One part fresh orange juice
- Two parts chilled champagne or dry sparkling wine

- Pour one-third of a champagne flute full of orange juice and top up with champagne. Stir gently, so as not to dissipate all the bubbles, and serve.
- For added fun, the champagne flute can have its rim frosted with sugar.

SOUTHERN CHAMPAGNE

Southern Comfort is a pleasantly warming drink that can be used in many combinations to create interesting cocktails. Here it is used to add a whole new dimension to dry champagne.

- Angostura bitters
- One shot glass of Southern Comfort
- Dry champagne
- Orange peel

- Splash a dash or two of Angostura bitters into a champagne flute and swirl it about to coat the inside.
- Pour in the Southern Comfort and top up with chilled dry champagne. Do not stir.
- Twist a length of orange peel over the drink to release the zest and then drop the peel into it as a garnish.

FUTURE
CLASSICS

Most drinkers tend to be rather conservative in their daily drinking habits, ordering the same drink and the same brand time after time. **Cocktails** have changed all that and people are now much more likely to be adventurous and try new tastes and new combinations of drinks.

The liquor industry is a vibrant and competitive one and new and **exciting concoctions** are released on the market every year. As can be expected, this brings an annual crop of new cocktails as bartenders around the world see what magic they can weave with the new flavours available to them. Some of these newcomers are great, others merely good.

Some of the **cocktails** on the following pages will enjoy a brief spell of fame and then fade from the scene forever. Others may eventually go on to become **classics** such as the Martini and the Harvey Wallbanger. We leave it to our readers to make up their minds as to which will stay around and which will fade from memory.

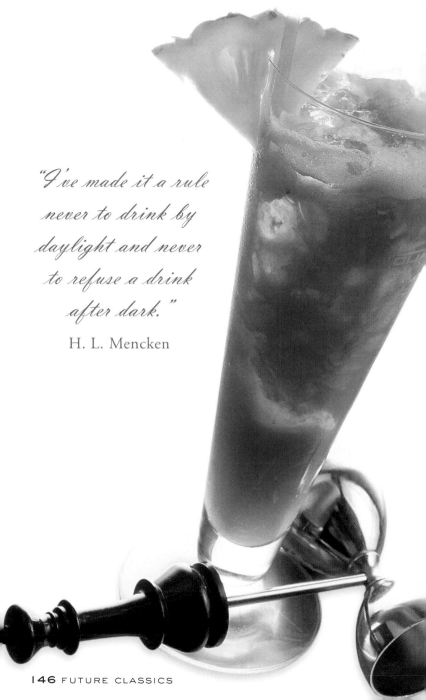

"I've made it a rule never to drink by daylight and never to refuse a drink after dark."

H. L. Mencken

FRANGELICO LUAU

Frangelico is reputed to have been created by an Italian hermit three centuries ago. It is a delicious liqueur made from hazelnuts and berries, used as a base for unusual and complex-flavoured cocktails like this one.

- One part Frangelico liqueur
- Four parts freshly made pineapple juice
- A dash of grenadine
- Ice cubes
- Fresh pineapple

° Pour Frangelico, pineapple juice and grenadine into a blender and blend for about 10 seconds. Pour into a chilled tall glass and add three ice cubes.
° Decorate with fresh pineapple.

Frangelico Luau is a rich combination of fruit, berry and nut flavours.

THE GREEK TIGER

This variation of the classic cocktail that is called Tiger Tail was offered to me on a ferry from Athens to Poros. The ship's steward insisted that it was the perfect way in which to introduce a foreigner to the delights of ouzo. I had to agree.

- Ice cubes
- Four parts fresh orange juice
- One part ouzo
- A slice of lime
- A twist of lime peel

° Place four ice cubes in a cocktail shaker and add the orange juice and ouzo.
° Shake well and strain into a cocktail glass.
° Squeeze the slice of lime over the drink and decorate it with a little lime peel.

THE PINK SQUIRREL

Any drink that has been flavoured with nut liqueur and decorated with nuts is likely to find itself branded as a squirrel's favourite.

- Crushed ice
- One part crème de noyaux or Frangelico liqueur
- One part crème de cacao
- One part thin cream
- Half a walnut

- Place a few spoons of crushed ice into your cocktail shaker or blender.
- Add the nut liqueur, crème de cacao and cream.
- Shake or blend the ingredients until thoroughly mixed.
- Strain into a cocktail glass.
- Decorate by floating a walnut half on the surface, and serve.

GOLDEN CADILLAC

Galliano has a vivid golden colour and a nutty-sweet flavour. The crème de cacao gives a smooth chocolaty flavour and the cream allows it to slip down like liquid velvet.

- Ice cubes
- One part Galliano
- One part crème de cacao
- One part thin cream

- Place three ice cubes in a cocktail shaker and add the Galliano, crème de cacao and fresh cream.
- Shake well and strain into a cocktail glass.
- Serve ungarnished.

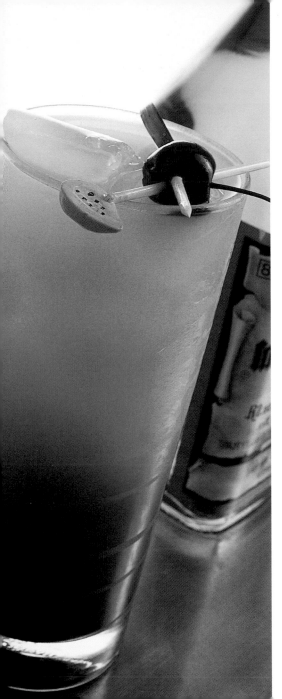

TEQUILA SUNRISE

Tequila, of course, is the beloved national drink of Mexico, and this cocktail is one of many based on the fiery spirit. It has become a cocktail classic.

- One part tequila
- Three parts fresh orange juice
- Two dashes of grenadine
- A maraschino cherry

Pour the tequila and orange juice into a highball glass and stir them well.

Splash grenadine on top of the mixture, close to the side of the glass, and watch the colour sink gently through the drink.

Garnish with a cherry spiked on a cocktail stick.

MARGARITA

Nobody remembers who Margarita was, but her name lives on in this fiery little drink that can be served straight up or frozen.

- Crushed ice
- Three parts tequila
- One part Triple Sec
- One part lime juice (preferably fresh)
- Salt
- Ice cubes

- Place a generous scoop of crushed ice in a blender or shaker and add the tequila, Triple Sec and lime juice. Blend or shake well.
- Dip the rim of a cocktail glass in egg white or lemon juice and frost with salt.
- Add two ice cubes and gently pour the Margarita mixture over them, taking care not to disturb the salt frosting.

THE GRASSHOPPER

This is a different and exciting drink, both in looks and flavour. The mint and coffee flavours are traditional meal-enders, so what better than combining them in an attractive drink?

The cream gives this well-rounded cocktail a silky texture.

- Ice cubes
- One part green crème de menthe
- One part crème de cacao
- One part thin cream

- Place three ice cubes in a cocktail shaker and add all the other ingredients.
- Shake well and strain into a cocktail glass.
- Serve ungarnished or with a sprig of mint.

*Golden Dream (**above left**) was invented when Galliano came onto the market in 1960. The smooth, minty flavour of the Grasshopper (**above right**) is just right to clear the palate after a good meal.*

GOLDEN DREAM

Bartenders and mixologists everywhere recognized Galliano's potential as a cocktail ingredient and there was a rush to see who could use it to best advantage. This delightful concoction certainly deserves an award for flavour and looks.

- Ice cubes
- Two parts Galliano
- One part Cointreau
- One part fresh orange juice
- One part thin cream

- Place three ice cubes in a cocktail shaker and then add the Galliano, Cointreau, orange juice and cream.
- Shake vigorously, then strain the contents into a cocktail glass.
- Serve ungarnished.

The Mexican Ruin is very good with coffee, or even instead of coffee.

MEXICAN RUIN

Tequila has probably been the ruin of many a Mexican, but this elegant variation should not leave too wide a trail of destruction in its wake.

- Crushed ice
- One part tequila
- One part coffee liqueur

- Place a scoop of crushed ice in a cocktail mixing glass.
- Add the tequila and coffee liqueur and stir well.
- Strain the mixture into a cocktail glass and serve.

MONTEZUMA

Mexico again, and this time it's a really unusual drink that looks good and tastes wonderful.

- Crushed ice (or ice cubes if using a shaker)
- One egg yolk
- Two parts tequila
- One part Madeira wine

- Place a scoop of crushed ice in a blender (or four ice cubes in a cocktail shaker) and add the egg yolk, tequila and Madeira wine.
- Blend for about 15 seconds, or shake very vigorously, and then strain the drink into a chilled cocktail glass.

TNT (TEQUILA 'N' TONIC)

Anything based on tequila is likely to produce interesting results. This one's not a drink for the faint-hearted.

- Ice cubes
- Two parts tequila
- Half a part fresh lime juice
- Tonic water
- Lemon peel

- Place three ice cubes in a bar glass, add the tequila and lime juice and stir well.
- Strain into a lowball glass, top up with tonic water and garnish with a twist of lemon peel.

*The Montezuma (**above left**), in which egg yolk is used to create a golden hue, and TNT (**above right**), the drink with a potentially explosive result.*

"We'll teach you to drink ere you depart."

William Shakespeare
Hamlet

DANISH MARY

In Scandinavian countries, a robust liquor called aquavit is made from potatoes or grain and lightly flavoured with caraway and other seeds. Traditionally it is swallowed neat in a single gulp, but can also be used in cocktails.

- Ice cubes
- One part aquavit
- One small can of tomato juice
- Two dashes of Worcestershire sauce
- Lemon juice
- Celery salt
- A celery stick

- Place four or five ice cubes in a cocktail shaker and add the aquavit, tomato juice, Worcestershire sauce, a few teaspoons of lemon juice and a dusting of celery salt.
- Shake well and strain into a highball glass.
- Garnish with the stick of celery and serve.

THE FROZEN MATADOR

Bullfighting usually takes place in the heat and dust of summer, so there is something rare and unusual about a frozen matador, just as there is about this very refreshing cocktail.

- Crushed ice
- One part tequila
- One part fresh pineapple juice
- A dash of fresh lime juice
- Ice cubes
- Slices of pineapple
- Mint leaves

- For this drink a blender is essential. Place two generous scoops of crushed ice in the blender and add the tequila, pineapple juice and lime juice. Blend to a frothy mixture.
- Strain into a lowball glass, add two ice cubes and garnish with the pineapple slices and the mint leaves.

The Frozen Matador (**opposite left**) *is a chilly concoction of tequila, pineapple and lime juice. Danish Mary* (**opposite right**) *is made with aquavit instead of vodka.*

SHOOTERS

Shooters add a bold splash of colour to any party. They're sassy and flashy and just a bit daring.

Originally invented by a Canadian barman to keep out the cold, **shooters** consist of small, high-powered drinks, usually built up in layers of contrasting colour and designed to be knocked back in one gulp. The art of making a shooter lies in getting each colour to be cleanly separated from the others. This requires some experimentation if you are to get it right every time, but practice makes perfect.

As a general rule, drinks with a **high alcohol** content are lighter than those with a lower alcohol content, so they will tend to float on top. In most countries it is required by law to state the alcohol content of the drink on the label, so this gives the budding bartender a good starting point.

This rule does not always apply, as some **drinks** have ingredients that are heavier than the alcohol, but it can be used as a general rule of thumb. It often helps to trickle the top layer onto the lower one by running the drink gently over the back of a teaspoon.

GALLIANO HOT SHOT

Galliano is a sweet, golden drink that goes well with the coffee or pudding at the end of a good meal. It seems natural to combine it with strong, bitter coffee to create this intriguing taste combination. If the coffee is very hot, it may be advisable to sip this drink, rather than tossing it back in a single gulp.

- One part Galliano
- One part very strong, hot coffee
- Thick cream

- Half fill a shot glass with Galliano and carefully trickle about the same quantity of hot coffee over the back of a teaspoon to form a dark layer on it.
- Finally, add a topping of cream, sliding it carefully onto the surface of the coffee.

CACTUS FLOWER

Here's a drink for the macho man. Keep a glass of iced water close at hand to douse any flames!

- Tabasco sauce
- Tequila

- Trickle a generous layer of Tabasco sauce onto the bottom of a shot glass.
- Carefully fill the glass with tequila, trying not to stir up the Tabasco.
- Toss back in a single gulp.

"I have taken more out of alcohol than it has taken out of me."

Winston Churchill

*The Galliano Hot Shot (**opposite front**) is an intriguing combination of Galliano and hot coffee, whereas the Cactus Flower (**opposite left**), a searing combination of tequila and Tabasco sauce, is best accompanied by a glass of iced water.*

LOVE BITE

A romantic little stinger for lovers.

- One part cherry liqueur
- One part parfait amour liqueur
- One part thick sweet cream

Pour the cherry liqueur into the bottom of a shot glass, filling it to about one-third. Carefully trickle the parfait amour onto the surface to fill the glass to about two-thirds.

Finally, slide a layer of sweet cream over the back of a spoon onto the surface and serve.

SLIPPERY NIPPLE

Who could resist a drink with a name as seductive as this?

- One part black sambuca
- One part Bailey's Irish Cream

○ Pour the sambuca into a shot glass, filling it to about the halfway mark.

○ Very carefully and slowly trickle the Bailey's Irish Cream onto the sambuca (over the back of a spoon) to fill the glass to the brim.

○ After admiring your beautiful handiwork, take a deep breath, raise the glass and then toss the contents back in a single, breathtaking gulp.

POUSSE CAFÉ

This is the original drink on which the shooter idea is based. The trick is to build it carefully, starting with the heaviest substance and pouring each subsequent one carefully over the back of a spoon so that the colours remain separate – until the glass is tilted for drinking. It demands a steady hand and is one of the very few drinks where looks are considered as important as flavour.

You could design your own using specially selected colours for particular occasions; the national colours of a country for a national holiday, or the colours of a football team's jerseys to celebrate a victory. Here's a typical pousse café to begin with.

- One part grenadine
- One part green crème de menthe
- One part Galliano
- One part kümmel
- One part brandy

• Pour each of the ingredients into a small, cylindrical glass in the order given, trickling them over a spoon onto the surface of the previous layer until a striped effect is achieved. Serve carefully.

AUTUMN LEAF

It doesn't matter too much if the colours blend a little. They will end up looking similar to the colour of an autumn leaf anyway.

- One part green crème de menthe
- One part Galliano
- One part brandy
- Grated nutmeg

- As with other shooters, use a small cylindrical glass and start by pouring in the crème de menthe.
- Now trickle the yellow Galliano carefully onto the surface of the green and end off by sliding a layer of golden brandy on top.
- Finish the drink off with a pinch of nutmeg.

Alan Mowbray pours a drink for Frances Dee in a scene from Nice Women.

THE SOMBRERO

Here is a cheerful little splash of Mexican magic to get you throwing your hat in the air.

- One part Kahlua
- One part thick cream

- Chill the Kahlua well.
- Pour the cold liqueur into a shot glass.
- Trickle the cream onto the Kahlua, letting it run over the back of a spoon.
- Serve with a steady hand.

It takes a steady hand to create a clean line between the ingredients of the Sombrero.

A SHOT OF FRENCH FIRE

A colourful little drink with a French flavour and a cheerful appearance.

- One part green chartreuse
- One part maraschino liqueur
- One part cherry brandy
- One part kümmel

- Starting with the chartreuse, trickle each of the ingredients over the back of a spoon into a small, straight-sided glass in the order shown.
- Admire for a few seconds, and toss it down in a single, multi-coloured gulp.

THE BASTILLE BOMB

Fire off this little shooter to celebrate the anniversary of the storming of the Bastille on 14 July 1789.

- One part grenadine
- One part blue Curaçao
- One part Cointreau

- Start with grenadine as a base in a small cylindrical glass, then trickle the Cointreau on top of it and round it off with a trickled layer of blue Curaçao. Voilá!

THE ANGEL'S TIT

It's not difficult to imagine how this creamy, smooth drink, decorated sensuously with a rounded cherry, derived its name. It's one of very few shooters served with a garnish.

- One part crème de cacao
- One part maraschino liqueur
- One part thick cream
- A maraschino cherry

- Starting with the crème de cacao, trickle each ingredient into a shooter glass in the order shown.
- Place a cherry in the cream layer and serve with reverence.

A Shot of French Fire (**above left**) *is a good test of dexterity to see whether you can keep the colours separate. In spite of its somewhat inelegant name, the Angel's Tit* (**above right**) *has become a classic.*

NON-ALCOHOLIC DRINKS

There are many reasons why some **party goers** prefer not to indulge in alcohol. It could be for religious or health reasons, or simply to have one member of the group **sober** enough to drive the rest home safely, and legally, at the end of the evening. There are also occasions when a party guest might be on some medication that does not combine safely with alcohol.

But these should not be reason to stay away from a party altogether, or to sit solemnly sipping a glass of water all evening. There are many safe and tasty **alcohol-free** cocktails that will provide pleasure without turning the drinker into a party-pooper.

With non-alcoholic drinks, as with any other drink, the **secret** is to find a good balance between sweetness and acidity. This is why Coco-Cola was such a universal **success**. It hit just the right balance and stayed with it. When designing any non-alcoholic drink, therefore, the bartender should aim for the same taste balances.

JUNGLE COOLER

Most fruit juices combine very well to form interesting new flavour combinations. This one is designed to capture the wild exotic character of a tropical jungle.

- Crushed ice
- Four parts pineapple juice
- Two parts fresh orange juice
- One part passion fruit squash (cordial)
- One part coconut milk
- A slice of pineapple

  Place a cup of crushed ice in a cocktail shaker and add the fruit juices as well as the coconut milk.

  Shake well to mix and then strain into a tall glass.

  Garnish with a slice of pineapple.

VIRGIN MARY

This drink is a Bloody Mary rendered innocent by the absence of alcohol.

- Ice cubes
- One can of tomato cocktail
- A small measure of lemon juice
- A dash of Tabasco sauce per glass
- A dash of Worcestershire sauce per glass
- Celery salt to taste
- Pepper
- A celery stick

  Place some ice cubes in a cocktail shaker and add the tomato cocktail and lemon juice.

  Add the seasoning as required and shake well.

  Strain into a tall glass and serve with the celery stick as a stirrer.

*Try different fruit juice combinations when making the Jungle Cooler (**opposite left**).*
*Sweet and simple, but delicious, a Virgin Mary (**opposite right**) contains no vodka.*

ORANGE FIZZ

The quantities can be varied according to the sweetness of the orange juice. If your mixture is too acidic, add a little sugar to correct the balance.

- Ice cubes
- One part fresh lime juice
- One part fresh lemon juice
- Five parts fresh orange juice
- Soda water
- Sugar to taste (if required)

Place four ice cubes in a cocktail shaker and add the three fruit juices.

Shake well and strain into a tall glass.

Top up with soda water and add a touch of sugar if it is too tart.

Serve ungarnished.

JONES'S BEACH COCKTAIL

Cocktails are not necessarily limited to sweet and sour flavours. Some, like the famous Bloody Mary, venture into the savoury taste spectrum. This is another savoury treat.

- Crushed ice
- A cup of cold beef consommé or a dissolved bouillon cube
- Half a cup of clam juice
- The juice of half a lemon or lime
- Half a teaspoon of horseradish sauce
- Two dashes of Worcestershire sauce

Fruit serves two important functions in a cocktail, it adds appearance and flavour. A slice of ripe fruit can provide a tangy touch to an otherwise uninspired drink.

- Place half a cup of crushed ice in a blender and add all ingredients except the celery salt.
- Blend for about 10 seconds and strain into a highball glass.
- Dust with a pinch of celery salt before serving.

"He that goes to bed thirsty rises healthy."

George Herbert

PUSSYFOOT

This tasty, fun drink should have you purring in no time at all.

- Ice cubes
- Two parts orange juice
- One part lemon juice
- Half an egg yolk per glass
- A dash of grenadine per glass
- A sprig of mint
- A cocktail cherry

Place four ice cubes in a cocktail shaker and pour all the liquid ingredients over them.

Shake vigorously and strain into a highball glass.

Serve garnished with a sprig of mint, slightly crushed to release the aroma, and a cherry.

*The Pussyfoot (**opposite**) probably got its name from its smooth, silky texture.*

CHERRY POP

Like all good cocktails, alcoholic or not, this one looks good and has a pleasing balance of sweetness and acidity. Vary the proportions to suit your own taste. That's what makes cocktail blending such fun.

- One part cherry syrup
- Half a part of fresh lemon juice
- One part fresh orange juice
- Ice cubes
- Soda water
- A slice of lemon
- One glacé cherry

Place the cherry syrup, lemon juice and orange juice in a cocktail shaker and add four cubes of ice.

Shake well and strain into a highball glass.

Top up with soda water and decorate with the slice of lemon and the cherry.

GENTLE SEA BREEZE

A pleasant and refreshing blend of two fruit juices that really is a treat.

- Crushed ice
- One part cranberry juice
- One part grapefruit juice
- Ice cubes
- A sprig of mint (optional)

  Place a cup of crushed ice in a blender or cocktail shaker (a blender is best). Add the juices and blend or shake until frothy.
  Pour into a highball glass, add two ice cubes and serve with a sprig of mint or ungarnished.

BLUE SPARK

Not long ago a catering friend came to me for advice. She had been asked to cater for the annual staff dinner of the national electricity supply organization and wanted a special cocktail for the occasion.

There were two problems: the theme colour for the evening was electric blue (naturally) and many of the staff members were Muslims, who don't drink alcohol for religious reasons. We spent an interesting hour trying various recipes and eventually settled on this one, of which we are both very proud.

- Crushed ice
- Half a teaspoon of blue food colouring
- Two dashes of Angostura bitters
- One part lychee juice
- Three parts lemonade
- A slice of lemon

  Place three spoons of crushed ice in a bar glass, pour in a splash of blue food colouring, the bitters and lychee juice.
  Add lemonade and stir gently so as not to lose all the bubbles.
  Strain into a lowball glass and garnish with a slice of lemon.

*Although the use of food colouring may be considered cheating by cocktail purists, the Blue Spark (**opposite right**) looks very dramatic and tastes wonderful. Here again, the principle of balancing sweet and sour comes to the fore to create the Gentle Sea Breeze (**opposite left**).*

Lew Ayres seems to have a weakness for beautiful girls armed with cocktails in My Weakness.

BLACK COW

In some parts of the world this cocktail is known as a "cola special".

• Two scoops of vanilla ice cream
• A bottle of root beer or cola

Place the ice cream in a highball glass, add the root beer or cola and stir gently.

Serve with a straw as well as a long spoon.

HONEYMOON COCKTAIL

After the wedding reception, bride and groom will probably want to keep a clear head as they start their life together.

- Crushed ice
- A generous part apple juice
- An equal part orange juice
- A squeeze of lime juice
- Two teaspoons of honey
- Orange peel
- Sugared cherries

- Place three spoons of crushed ice in a cocktail shaker and add the apple and orange juice, squeeze of lime juice and honey.
- Shake well and strain into two champagne flutes.
- Garnish with a spiral of orange peel and a cherry.
- Serve in bed.

HONEYSWEET COFFEE

While most cocktails are designed to be enjoyed in the evening, here's one that's fine for any time of day. It even goes well with breakfast.

- A teaspoon of clear honey
- One mug of freshly brewed, strong coffee
- A dash of Angostura bitters
- Ice cubes
- Whipped cream
- Grated nutmeg

- Place the honey in the mug of coffee, stir well and allow to chill overnight.
- Add the bitters. Now place three ice cubes in a cocktail shaker, add the chilled coffee mixture and shake well.
- Strain into a highball glass and float whipped cream on top.
- Dust with a pinch of grated nutmeg and serve.

SHIRLEY TEMPLE

A good drink for anybody who enjoys a really sweet concoction.

- Ginger ale
- Grenadine syrup
- Maraschino cherries

- Fill a highball glass with ginger ale and add a splash or two of grenadine syrup.
- Stir very gently and drop in three red maraschino cherries.
- Serve with a straw.

"For when the wine is in, the wit is out."

Thomas Becon

Named after the child actress, the Shirley Temple (**opposite left**) *became the non-alcoholic cocktail of the 1960s. Honeysweet Coffee* (**opposite right**) *makes a delicious, early-morning drink.*

CATHERINE BLOSSOM COCKTAIL

This cocktail is deliciously tangy and clean-tasting.

- Crushed ice
- One cup of freshly squeezed orange juice
- Two spoons of maple syrup
- A dash of lemon juice
- A twist of lemon peel

Place two scoops of crushed ice in a blender and add the juices and maple syrup.

Blend well and pour into a highball glass.

Garnish with a twist of lemon peel and serve.

Safe Sex on the Beach (**opposite left**) *is every bit as delicious as the "real thing" while taking away that morning-after worry. The Catherine Blossom* (**opposite right**) *became a classic in the cocktail world as one of the old favourites in the safe drinking list.*

SAFE SEX ON THE BEACH

Like many non-alcoholic cocktails, this one is simply a version of a tried-and-tested recipe, but without the alcohol. Sex on the Beach uses vodka and fruit schnapps. To make it "safe", leave out the vodka and replace the schnapps with fruit nectar.

- Ice cubes
- One part peach nectar
- Three parts pineapple juice
- Three parts orange juice
- A squeeze of fresh lime juice
- A twist of lime peel
- A slice of kiwi fruit
- A strawberry

Place four ice cubes in a cocktail mixing glass and add the peach nectar (usually a blend of peach juice with other, deflavoured fruit juice bases), the pineapple juice, orange juice and the squeeze of lime juice.

Stir it well and strain the mixture into a tall glass.

Add fresh ice and garnish with a twist of lime peel, a slice of kiwi fruit and a strawberry.

GLOSSARY

As with any specialized activity, so cocktail mixing and bartending, too, have developed a particular vocabulary. While jargon has been kept to a bare minimum in this book, it is good to know what people mean when they refer to a 'straight up' or *digestif*. Here are some of the more commonly used cocktail terms.

Apéritif: A drink served before a meal to stimulate appetite. Traditional apéritifs include fino sherry and brut champagne. Some cocktails are made dry for the same reason.

Bar syrup: A sweetening agent, usually made by mixing three parts sugar and one part water. A well-equipped bar always has a bottle of ready-made bar syrup handy.

Blend: In the modern cocktail bars an electric blender has become standard equipment. It is particularly useful when fresh fruit has to be puréed as part of a drink. To blend a drink thoroughly, run the machine for only about 10 seconds.

Dash: A dash of something is simply a small amount splashed into the glass. Very strong flavours, such as bitters, sauces or syrups, are commonly added in dashes.

Digestif: A small and usually quite sweet drink that is served at the end of a meal to aid the digestion.

Flip: A short drink that is mixed with egg (and sometimes sugar) and then shaken into a smooth froth. A single egg is often too rich for just one flip, and it is difficult to separate an egg into two, so it is easiest to make them two at a time.

Float: To pour a small amount of liquor or cream on top of a cocktail so it does not mix with the rest of the ingredients. This is often done by trickling it over the back of a spoon.

Frappé: A frappé is a drink made by pouring a sweet liqueur over crushed ice. It is served with a straw, so the melting ice and liqueur are sipped together from the bottom of the glass. *See* also Mist.

Frosting: Glasses can be frosted by wetting the rim with water or egg white and dipping it into sugar, which then clings to the rim. Margaritas are traditionally served in glasses frosted with salt instead of sugar.

Jigger: A small measure used in making cocktails. The American jigger contains 1.5 ounces, or 42.3 cc. There are also one-ounce and two-ounce jiggers.

Mist: A straight (or neat) alcoholic liquor that is simply poured over crushed ice. The mist is related to the frappé (*see* above), which is a sweet liqueur poured over crushed ice.

Muddle: Herbs, such as mint, are sometimes muddled to release the juices and flavour. This is done by placing them at the bottom of a glass and crushing them to a smooth paste using a wooden pestle, so as not to scratch the glass. Sometimes bar spoons are made with a flat disc at the end of the long handle. This is designed to be used as a muddler.

Mulled: A drink served hot and often enjoyed in winter. Originally drinks like ale and wine were warmed by plunging a hot poker into the tankard. As hot pokers are a rarity today, the drinks are simply warmed over a stove or hot plate.

Neat: Alcohol served without any mixer or ice. In Scandinavian countries, aquavit is often drunk neat.

On the rocks: Alcohol poured over ice cubes. Often a glass is filled to the top with ice cubes. This method serves a double purpose: it dilutes the liquor slightly and chills it.

Punch: A punch is made of liquor and fruits and served from a punch bowl at a large gathering. It's a sort of bulk-delivered cocktail.

Shake: To pour the ingredients into a cocktail shaker with some ice and shake it vigorously to ensure a good blend. The ice acts as a beater and dilutes it slightly.

Spiral: Sometimes a drink calls for a garnish that is described as a "spiral" of orange or lemon peel. This is peel cut from the fruit in a thin, long and even strip and used to decorate and flavour the drink.

Straight up: Served without ice, usually in a tall glass.

Strain: After shaking or stirring a drink, you usually want to separate the liquid from the ice or peel or other solid ingredients. To do this, the drink is poured through a strainer. Good bars have specially designed strainers that fit snugly over their shakers or mixing glasses.

Swizzle stick: A stirrer, sometimes made of silver, ivory or wood, but today mostly made of plastic. It acts as a decoration for the drink and can also be used to stir it from time to time. Many liquor companies provide swizzle sticks that bear the company logo or crest on the top.

Twist: A long piece of peel (usually citrus) that is twisted in the middle to release the tangy oil from the outer zest layer. It is then dropped into the drink as a garnish.

Zest: The very outside part of the citrus peel. It is obtained by cutting it off with a sharp knife or vegetable peeler. Zest does not include the soft white part (pith) of the skin.

INDEX

Note: figures in **bold** indicate that the entries appear in photographs.

PHOTOGRAPHIC CREDITS

ABPL: pp. 10 and 11. Photofest: pp.8, 18, 48, 73, 89, 131, 166, 180

PUBLISHER'S ACKNOWLEDGEMENTS

The photographer and the publishers wish to thank Banks Hiring Supply SA, Buying Service SA (Pty) Ltd, Spilhaus WM Silverware (Pty) Ltd and The Yellow Door for their generosity in supplying the glassware for the photography.

"There are two reasons for drinking: one is when you are thirsty, to cure it, the other is when you are not thirsty, to prevent it."

Thomas Love Peacock